HOW TO WIN IN TRAFFIC COURT

How to WIN IN TRAFFIC COURT

The Non-Lawyers Guide to
Successfully Defending Traffic Violations

UNITED STATES EDITION

PHIL BELLO, J.D.

MAJOR MARKET
B O O K S

Gibbsboro, New Jersey

QUANTITY SALES

This book is available at quantity discounts for corporations, organizations, and special interest groups. For information, please contact Sales Dept., Major Market Books, 146 S. Lakeview Dr., Ste. 300, Gibbsboro, NJ 08026

INDIVIDUAL SALES

To order copies of this book simply send a check or money order for $12.95 per copy plus shipping ($2.00 for the first book plus 75¢ for each additional book) Mail to: Major Market Books, P.O. Box 175, Gibbsboro, NJ 08026.

Library of Congress Catalog Card Number: 89-50401

ISBN 1-877635-38-3

First Edition

Printed in the United States of America

DEDICATED to all of the motorists
across the nation
who never had a fighting chance
in traffic court.

This Book Belongs To: Mark Mour

CONTENTS

ACKNOWLEDGMENTS

My sincere thanks go to my family and my friends, who lent me encouragement and support during the course of writing this book.

With special thanks to:

Barbara Morgan (typing)
Julie Byrnes (proofreading)
Roger Egan (editing)
Anne O'Donnell (interior design)
Anita Curry (cover design)
Multifacit Graphics, Inc. (typesetting)
Barbara Farabaugh (indexing)
Kingsway Studio (cover photo)

PERMISSIONS:
Subpoena forms are reprinted with permission from Julius Blumberg, Inc.

Materials from the Nebraska Revised Statutes are reprinted with permission of the Revisor of Statutes, Nebraska Unicameral Legislature.

Materials in Figure 10.3 and Appendix B are reprinted with permission of the National Safety Council.

Figure 11.2 is reprinted with permission from Connecticut General Statutes Annotated, Copywright © 1987 By West Publishing Co.

Materials from the Delaware Code Annotated, as amended, are reprinted with permission of The Michie Company.

Materials from the New Jersey Administrative Code are reprinted with permission from the State of New Jersey, Office of Administrative Law.

INTRODUCTION

During the course of more than a decade of trying cases in traffic court, I've noticed something—the majority of motorists who appear, do so *without* the assistance of an attorney. While some of these individuals attempt to defend themselves, many more simply admit responsibility for their offense without making any effort to fight their case. I would venture to say that many of those who don't bother to fight their traffic tickets are under the false impression that winning their cases is hopeless. Not true! *The truth is that there are many ways to win in traffic court, but they are relatively unknown to most American motorists.* What bothers me the most about such cases is that many people across the nation are needlessly suffering the consequences of traffic court convictions, which include heavy fines, soaring insurance rates, the loss of driving privileges, and even imprisonment.

I'd like to make it clear that this book is aimed at reaching those of you who cannot afford an attorney or have decided not to hire one for whatever reasons. It certainly is not my intention to deter you from seeking legal counsel if that is your desire. Since attorneys have had legal training, it is obvious and only logical that their ability to handle a case in traffic court would most likely surpass that of someone without any training in the law. Nevertheless, when it comes to traffic tickets, the majority of motorists choose to represent themselves without an attorney. In my opinion, one of the major reasons for this is that a lot of people just can't afford to pay the legal fee.

In some situations, it may be possible to have an attorney appointed free of charge if you can't afford one, especially for more serious traffic offenses. So, if you are afforded this opportunity, you should by all means apply for an attorney. *But the awful truth is that, though you may want legal representation, you don't have a right to a free attorney in most cases, even if you can't afford one!* If this is your situation (and it is for many motorists), your choice will be limited to either (1) admitting responsibility for the offense, or (2) representing yourself at trial without an attorney.

If you decide to fight your ticket without legal representation you *must* know what you are doing. Without the necessary information, your chances of winning are about as good as hitting the bull's-eye in a dart game while blindfolded. That's why this book was written. It was written to take much of the "mystery" out of a traffic hearing by explaining the basics simply and without "legalese." As you read through its pages, you will discover many techniques, strategies, and approaches, any one of which could be the "ticket" you need to win your case.

Even if you hire an attorney, however, this book can be beneficial for a couple of reasons. First, it will show how you can put your ideas across more persuasively when you testify. Also, once you know the rules of the game, you can function as a better teammate with your attorney.

This book is addressed primarily to the majority of jurisdictions in the United States that treat traffic offenses as essentially formal proceedings in court. Therefore, some of the information may not be applicable, especially in the minority of jurisdictions in which traffic cases are heard informally or by administrative agencies.

In addition, since each individual traffic court is subject to its own laws and local customs, the information presented here may be affected to a small degree. Most of the information, however, should come in handy in the vast majority of situations.

As you read this book, bear in mind that various jurisdictions sometimes use different terminology to describe essentially the same function or procedure in a traffic hearing. For example, the individual who presides at trial in many jurisdictions is commonly referred to as the "judge." In other jurisdictions, however, he may also be referred to by such titles as a "magistrate," or a "referee." In like manner, various terms such as "statutes" or "codes" are used to designate the volumes where the traffic laws can be found, e.g., the Vermont Statutes Annotated or the Tennessee Code Annotated. In order to avoid any confusion, therefore, I have, for the most part, used only one designation for any given term or phrase throughout the book. However, you should understand that the terminology that is used here is intended to be interchangeable and equivalent to the terminology used in your particular jurisdiction. Whenever you are in doubt as to the meaning of any term or phrase, I suggest that you refer to the definitions that appear at the back of this book or to a legal dictionary for clarification.

Besides differences in terminology, there are other variations among jurisdictions that should be noted. For example, in most locations throughout the United States, a judge hears traffic matters, yet in a few jurisdictions, certain traffic offenses are heard by juries, with a judge presiding. Some courts have a prosecutor who presents cases on the state's behalf, while others don't. Differences such as these, however, should not affect the applicability or usefulness of what is said here to any significant degree.

Let me also take this opportunity to give you a word of advice: Always show respect for the police and cooperate with them if you are stopped for a traffic violation. This may sound simple and seem obvious, but you are much better off *avoiding* a ticket rather than having to defend one. However, if the need to defend yourself arises, you will come to realize that there is indeed much that you can do. By making use of the information and strategies provided in this book, there is no doubt that you can greatly improve your chances of winning your case in traffic court! I wish you the best of luck!

PHIL BELLO, J.D.

P.S. A final word:

For narrative simplicity, I have used the male pronoun throughout this book. No offense is intended to my female colleagues, judges, police personnel, and, of course, my female readers.

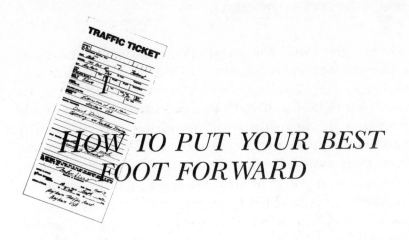

HOW TO PUT YOUR BEST FOOT FORWARD

I am sure you know that it's necessary to make a good impression in traffic court. You may not realize, however, just how important it is to exhibit a pleasant attitude, good manners, and a neat and clean appearance. I say this because it is likely that the judge will rely on these things when he evaluates your credibility. A quote made by the English statesman, Lord Chesterfield, pretty well sums this up: "To please people is a great step toward persuading them."

In this respect, I have listed below some important guidelines that should assist you in making an attractive overall impression. Some require preparation; all should be followed closely.

1. Look neat and clean.
2. Address the judge by his proper title, such as "Your Honor," or "Judge."
3. Speak loudly and clearly when addressing the judge or others in court.
4. Listen carefully to questions that the judge or prosecutor may ask you, and be responsive to them.
5. Don't be late for your hearing.
6. Don't speak to other people so as to disrupt the proceedings.

7. Don't lose your cool or argue with the judge or prosecutor.

Incidentally, the merits in your traffic case may be so close that the decision could go either way. In such a situation, your appearance, manners, and attitude are especially important. Who knows, if you make a good overall impression, it could be just enough to tilt the scales of justice in your favor. (I'm convinced that there were more than a few occasions where I've won cases simply because my client was polite and well-dressed. This may not be saying much for the idea of "blind justice," but it's the truth.)

It should be mentioned here that you can be held in contempt of court if you engage in disruptive conduct, vulgar language, or insulting behavior. Besides the possibility of being fined and even imprisoned, this type of behavior has an extremely negative impact on the judge and it should be avoided at all costs. Also, you can be held in contempt of court if you fail to show up in court when your hearing is scheduled. In most jurisdictions, the judge can issue an arrest warrant in order to get you into court. In other jurisdictions, your failure to appear might result in losing your case by default. Needless to say, it doesn't make any sense to risk losing your case by not showing. You should mark down the date and time of your hearing and clear your schedule of any conflicting engagements. It is one thing to lose your case after trying it and after giving it your best effort. At least you've gone down fighting. But to lose by default, without having your "day in court," is a real shame.

If for any reason you are going to be late for court, you should phone the court clerk and tell him about the delay. Then if your case is called before you get to court, the judge should not hold you in contempt. Furthermore, even though the judge may not like the fact that you are late, he should nonetheless be favorably impressed by the fact that you showed enough courtesy to call.

KNOW YOUR RIGHTS

One of the greatest things about our system of American justice is its provision that all individuals be treated fairly. This is evidenced by the Fourteenth Amendment to the United States Constitution that provides: "Nor shall any State deprive any person of life, liberty or property, without due process of law." In the context of a traffic court hearing, this means that certain specific rights are given to motorists in order to insure a fair hearing.

In this chapter, we will take a look at those rights that, for the most part, will apply to you as a defendant in traffic court. Keep in mind, however, that the nature and extent of the rights given in traffic courts vary somewhat among the states. This is largely due to the fact that some states have decriminalized some traffic offenses, while others treat them essentially in the nature of a crime. In other words, since the Constitution affords a large degree of protection to individuals accused of crimes, you will generally be afforded more rights if you live in a state that regards a traffic offense as a criminal or quasi-criminal proceeding.

PRESUMPTION OF INNOCENCE

Voltaire, the French historian and writer, once said that "it is better to risk saving a guilty man than to condemn an innocent one." The philosophy behind this concept reflects the American tradition that persons accused of crimes are always presumed to be innocent until they are proven guilty. In like manner, this tradition also applies to traffic offenses. Fortunately, as a defendant in traffic court, you don't have to prove your innocence. INDEED, IT'S ALWAYS THE STATE'S JOB TO BEAR THE BUR- DEN OF PROVING YOUR GUILT. Remember this, be- cause it's probably the single most important concept in this book.

If your offense occurs in one of the majority of states that regards traffic offenses as being a criminal or quasi-criminal proceeding, the amount of proof generally needed to convict you is "beyond a reasonable doubt." In other jurisdictions, however, standards that require a lesser degree of proof may be used. Such standards are usually referred to as "clear and convincing evidence," or a "preponderance of the evidence." The point is that whatever standard the court uses to establish your guilt, the state *must* supply enough evidence to meet that stand- ard. If it fails to do this, it is the duty of the court to dismiss the proceeding against you. Essentially, then, your goal is to create doubt in the judge's mind and thereby cause him to believe that the state has fallen short of meeting the standard of proof. If you can do that, you should be victorious. As you read through the pages of this book, you will discover that there are many strategies and techniques that you can employ in order to accom- plish this goal.

REPRESENTATION BY COUNSEL

If you are accused of a traffic offense, you have the right to either engage an attorney or to represent yourself. Generally speaking, if you can't afford an attorney, you have the right to a free attorney at public expense *only* when there is a possibility that you will be imprisoned. In fact, since the the penalties for most traffic offenses don't involve the possibility of imprisonment, there is usually *no* right to a free attorney in traffic court. Hence, you may very well find yourself in a situation where you have only two choices; to defend yourself or to plead guilty.

I'm a great believer in people who "stick up" for their rights. By the same token, I don't think that defendants should plead guilty just because they don't know how to go about representing themselves. Indeed, that's why I wrote this book.

OBTAINING A CONTINUANCE

If you were forced to try your case without having a sufficient amount of time to prepare for it, you just might not fare very well. This would be patently unfair. That is why due process guarantees you a "reasonable" amount of time in which to prepare your defense. What this boils down to is that it's usually possible to obtain a continuance (postponement) of your case *if* you have a good reason.

What is considered to be a good reason to ask for a continuance? Courts will naturally differ in their view on this, however, I would venture to say that a medical emergency, for example, would almost always suffice. On the other hand, a social activity or even a planned vacation may not be satisfactory.

If you are successful in getting your hearing continued, there is generally no "set" amount of additional time you will receive. Usually, it varies with the circumstances of the case. The new hearing date may be a day later, or it may be months later. Of course, a lot may depend on the time schedule of the police officer or other witnesses who will be testifying for the state. There is further discussion on this subject in Chapter 4.

ENTERING YOUR PLEA

At some point after you have been issued a traffic ticket, you will be given the opportunity to enter a plea (e.g., guilty or not guilty) to the offense you have been charged with. *If you plead guilty (or accept responsibility), you are giving up your right to a hearing, as well as the important constitutional rights that accompany a hearing.* In my view, it's usually a big mistake to do this, especially if you have a good case. Why not take advantage of the presumption of innocence you enjoy as an American citizen and make the state prove its case against you? Since the state must satisfy a standard that requires a high degree of proof, there is *always* a chance that you will win. In fact, you may not realize just how good your chances are!

BRINGING WITNESSES TO YOUR HEARING

As a defendant in traffic court, you have the right to call witnesses to testify in your own behalf. Assuming that there are witnesses who are available and willing to testify for you, it's often a good idea to bring them to court. In other words, witnesses can lend support to your version of the facts and thereby strengthen your case.

Normally, any passengers who were with you at the time of the incident will make good witnesses. This is because they're usually familiar with the pertinent details, not to mention the fact that they are almost always sympathetic with your position. You shouldn't overlook the possibility of bringing to court any pedestrians who were witnesses to the incident. Don't forget, however, that it's important to determine first whether they support your position, and find out if they are willing to testify for you at trial. Incidentally, be sure to take down their names, addresses, and phone numbers, so that you can contact them or serve them with a subpoena if necessary.

I should mention that even though there may be no witnesses you know of, it doesn't necessarily mean that no one witnessed the incident. Actually, it's always possible that there is a witness who would be willing to help you out in court. In fact, such witnesses (who are often complete strangers), are generally more credible than friends or relatives. This is because they are less likely to be prejudiced in your favor. Consequently, judges usually give their testimony more "weight." Hence, if you think your case warrants it, you might want to place an ad in the newspaper requesting anyone who witnessed the incident that led to your traffic ticket to contact you. I've used this technique myself a few times with some success.

I should also add that the more witnesses you bring to court, the better off you usually are. I know this sounds simple, but the side that has the most credible witnesses usually wins. Moreover, I would suggest that you always bring witnesses to court if you have them. Actually, I've seen some situations where the state won its case despite the fact that defense witnesses outnumbered prosecution witnesses, but I'm sure this occurred because the defendant's witnesses were not believable. As you will see in Chapter 4, you can maximize your witnesses' credibility by preparing them before they go to court.

Furthermore, you should be aware that juveniles can make good witnesses. If the youngster is old enough to understand the obligation to tell the truth and has a positive contribution to make, you should certainly consider bringing him to the hearing.

Testifying in Your Own Defense

As a defendant in traffic court, you always have the right to testify in your own defense. You also have the right *not* to testify (the right to remain silent), except possibly in some jurisdictions that treat traffic offenses as civil rather than criminal proceedings.

Now you might ask the question: "What should I do, testify or remain silent? Well, if you believe that your story will move the judge to favor your side, naturally it's a good idea to testify. On the other hand, if you think that testifying will do you more harm than good, you might be better off to forget it. Again, since it's the state's obligation to prove its case against you, it's entirely possible in most situations to simply remain silent and still win your case.

Here's something else to consider: if you decide to testify, the state will be entitled to cross-examine you. If you don't testify, you can't be cross-examined. Thus, you may be better off not testifying if you think that you might say something that will damage your case during the state's cross-examination.

It is said that courts can't use a person's exercise of the right against self-incrimination as an indication of guilt. This may be true, but I believe that when a motorist elects to remain silent, it often has a negative impact on the judge. Wouldn't a motorist who believes that he is innocent of the charges against him have something to say in his own behalf? I think so. This is why I advise my clients to testify whenever they can present persuasive evidence in their own behalf.

CROSS-EXAMINING THE OPPOSITION

Another one of the rights you are guaranteed under the Constitution is the right of confrontation. This means that you can cross-examine any witness the state calls to testify against you at trial.

As you see in Chapter 6, cross-examination is one of the most effective tools you have at your disposal.

APPEAL

An appeal is the procedure by which a higher court reviews the decision of the traffic court. In most cases, you will have the right to appeal if the verdict has gone against you. Depending on your jurisdiction and the facts of your case, an appeal can involve a new trial, or simply a review of the record made at the original hearing.

Further discussion of this subject is contained in Chapter 12.

A GOOD OFFENSE CAN SOMETIMES BE YOUR BEST DEFENSE

You may not realize it, but you can have a traffic ticket issued against another motorist if you have knowledge and/or information that the motorist has committed a traffic violation. In other words, the right to file a traffic complaint is not confined solely to law enforcement officers.

The question naturally arises: why should you bring a complaint against another driver? The answer is that it can work to your advantage in a situation where you, instead of the actual wrongdoer, have been mistakenly charged with a traffic violation. To illustrate, consider a hypothetical situation. Let's assume that you were involved in a motor vehicle accident at an intersection with another driver, whom we will call Mr. Unfriendly. Imagine that the investigating police officer arrived at the scene about five minutes after the accident. Based on what he heard from Mr. Unfriendly, he charged you with going through a red light and causing an accident. The true story, however, is that Mr. Unfriendly went through the red light. In other words, *he* is the one who should have been charged with the offense.

Now, if *you* sign a complaint against Mr. Unfriendly for going through the red light, it's always possible that the court hearing will show that he was in the wrong instead of you. In fact, you might have the opportunity to cross-examine him and establish that he is the guilty party. So the end result may turn out that Mr. Unfriendly is found guilty and your charge is dismissed. Obviously, if you had never signed a complaint against him, you would be in court defending the charge solely on your own.

You should also think about the psychological aspect in this situation. For example, if you don't sign a complaint against Mr. Unfriendly, yet you testify that it was he who unlawfully ran the red light, the judge may wonder why you didn't complain. In other words, he may think that if you were truly innocent, it would be a natural human response for you to point your finger at the wrongdoer. The conclusion is clear: don't be the "fall guy" for someone else. If the police should have given someone else a traffic ticket but didn't, you can (and should) do something about it.

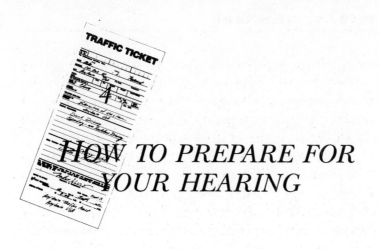

HOW TO PREPARE FOR YOUR HEARING

NOTIFYING THE COURT OF YOUR PLEA

Prior to your traffic hearing, you should let the court know that you will be contesting your case. This is necessary if you want to fight your ticket because the state has the right to be notified so that it can prepare its case against you.

If you don't notify the court or you notify it too late, you may wind up inconveniencing yourself. Suffice it to say that if you show up at your hearing and the state is unprepared (because you failed to give notice), you will no doubt be required to return to court another time. Therefore, I suggest that you notify the court that you will be pleading not guilty as soon as possible after you receive your ticket. This can save you a ton of inconvenience.

Probably the best way to notify the court of your plea is by sending a letter to the court. This way, you can make a copy of the letter for yourself and have it handy should it ever be necessary for you to prove that you sent notice.

A sample letter is shown in Figure 4.1, should you wish to use it as a model when you compose your own. (Notice that it contains a request for "discovery," which is discussed in the next section.)

To: Court Clerk
      Name and address of Traffic Court

Re: Your name
      Traffic Ticket #
      Date of offense

Dear Sir/Madam:

Please be advised that I am pleading not guilty to the above
referenced offense and will be representing myself pro se at
the court hearing which is presently scheduled for (date).

I would appreciate your sending me the following information:

1.   Police report.

2.   Statements of the state's witnesses.

3.   Any and all reports, test results, certifications, or other
     written documents pertaining to my offense that I am legally
     entitled to obtain by way of discovery.

Thank you for your cooperation.

Very Truly Yours,

(Your signature)

P.S. Should there be any change in the hearing date, I would
      appreciate your notifying me as soon as possible so that
      I can make arrangements to re-schedule my time accordingly.

FIGURE 4.1   NOTIFICATION OF PLEA AND REQUEST FOR DISCOVERY

I should also mention that the court clerk is usually
the appropriate person to address your letter to, but this
may vary. Therefore, it's a good idea to call the court first
in order to find out to whom you should address your
letter. Incidentally, when you call, ask for the name of the
person you speak with. Then if you have the need to call
back at a later time, you will be able to contact that individual directly.

OBTAINING DISCOVERY

Prior to your hearing, it may be possible for you to acquire information in the state's file that relates to your case. This process is known as "discovery." Such information can be very helpful in preparing your defense. The following items are examples of the type of information that may be available to you:

1. Police reports
2. Statements of witnesses
3. Certifications and reports relating to the accuracy of radar units or breath-testing instruments
4. Certifications and reports relating to the training or qualifications of police officers to operate radar units or breath-testing instruments

This kind of information can really give you an edge in your defense. For example, if you have the opportunity to read the statements of the state's witnesses, you can find out what they are likely to say when they testify at trial. This will certainly help you in your plan to cross-examine them. Here is another example of the usefulness of discovery. If you were charged with speeding, you could benefit tremendously by checking the certifications and reports regarding the accuracy of the radar unit and the training of the operator. If these documents were not in compliance with regulations, you might be able to block the state from introducing evidence of your speed at trial.

Discovery can also be a helpful tool if you intend to negotiate a plea bargain. (Note: See Chapter 5 for a discussion of plea bargaining.) In essence, if the information you obtain shows that the state has a weak case, you are put in a better bargaining position. This means that you can usually get a better deal.

I should mention that the information in the state's file is not usually sent automatically, so you'll most likely have to request it. The best way I have found to do this is to send a letter requesting *all* of the information that you are legally entitled to. Figure 4.1 contains a request for discovery that you may wish to use as a model when you compose your own.

LOOKING UP THE LAW

It is essential that you check the section of the State Vehicle Code or local ordinance that describes the offense you are charged under. In fact, trying to fight a ticket without knowing the law is something like trying to get an A in a college course without using a textbook. The reason for this is that the law provides the tools that are necessary to build your defense.

By analyzing the exact wording of the appropriate section of the law, you will get to see what conduct is made illegal. *By comparing your own conduct with the conduct that is illegal, you may discover that you have a valid defense.*

For example, suppose that you were charged with making an illegal U-turn in a residential district under California law. (Note: See Section 22103 of West's Annotated California Codes, which has been reproduced in Figure 4.2.) Referring to the wording of that statute, you will see that making a U-turn is only illegal under certain

---

§ **22103.** **U-turn in residence district**

No person in a residence district shall make a U-turn when any other vehicle is approaching from either direction within 200 feet, except at an intersection when the approaching vehicle is controlled by an official traffic control device.

FIGURE 4.2 WEST'S ANNOTATED CALIFORNIA CODES

circumstances. In other words, you would have a legal defense if you could demonstrate that there were no vehicles approaching within 200 feet at the time you made your U-turn. The point is this: you might not be aware of this defense if you had never bothered to look up the law!

To find out the section number of the statute or ordinance you are charged under, simply check your traffic ticket. Chances are that it will be written somewhere on the ticket. If you don't see it, though, you might try contacting the court clerk for this information. Once you have the section number, then it's just a matter of going to your local library or to a law library and looking it up in the appropriate set of books.

Since this book deals with a wide variety of topics, no attempt has been made to treat the area of legal research in any detail. Indeed, it would not be practical to do so in a book of this size. But you have the choice of either hiring someone to do it for you (e.g., a paralegal or a law student), or doing it yourself.

If you decide to do the research yourself, don't let the task frighten you. Actually, most traffic cases don't require extensive legal research. In the usual case, all that's necessary is to look up the applicable code or ordinance section, and you might be able to locate the specific information you are seeking simply by asking the librarian for some help. There may be occasions, however, when it is advisable or necessary to do some additional research into the law, especially in the more serious cases such as driving under the influence or driving while suspended. If this is the case, a librarian may not be able to give you all the help you need. Accordingly, I have listed a few excellent books in Appendix A that explain how to do legal research. They are all written on a level that is easy to understand and should give you no trouble should you wish to use any one of them.

USING EXHIBITS

The familiar cliche, "A picture is worth a thousand words," often applies in traffic court, in the sense that an exhibit can be enormously helpful in enabling you to get your point across clearly. Of course, not all cases will lend themselves to the use of exhibits. However, as a general rule of thumb, if it's difficult to describe something without a visual image of it, you should at least consider using an exhibit.

In order for an exhibit to have any value at your hearing, it's important that it depicts *accurately* what it is supposed to. For example, if you are sketching a diagram, try to draw it to scale as closely as possible and show the exact locations of vehicles and their directions of travel. Likewise, if you are taking photographs, make sure that they show a complete perspective, which may best be achieved by photographs from different angles.

It's also a good idea to take pictures or make your sketch as soon after the incident as possible, because your objective is to show the physical facts as they existed *at the time* of the incident. For example, it might be an integral part of your defense to show the location of certain signs posted along the roadway. If they are torn down by the time you take your pictures, you would certainly be at a disadvantage.

Using an exhibit at trial can be favorable from a psychological standpoint as well. I would venture to say that the vast majority of motorists don't bother going to the trouble of drawing a sketch or taking photographs when they present their cases in court. So, if you go into court well prepared with exhibits, you will no doubt earn more respect from the judge for doing so. This could make a big difference.

Chapter 7 takes a closer look at how an exhibit can be introduced in court.

USING SUBPOENAS

If you want to make sure that your witnesses show up in court, it's a good idea to serve them with a subpoena. A witness will usually think twice about missing a court hearing if he has been served with a subpoena because he faces a potential penalty if he ignores it. Don't forget that even though a witness may promise you that he will attend your hearing, it's possible that he may not show up for one reason or another. Of course, it may not be necessary to subpoena your spouse or a close relative. But unless you are sure a witness will show up, it's better to be safe than sorry. Needless to say, if you are lacking one or more witnesses at your hearing, you will be at a disadvantage.

Of course, even if subpoenaed, your witnesses may not show up. However, the fact that you have subpoenaed them can work to your advantage. For example, let's say you discover that your witnesses are not present in court. In such a situation, you would probably want to have another chance to get your witnesses into court rather than to try the case without them—you would probably want a continuance. Now, if the judge knows that you have subpoenaed your witnesses, he is much more likely to grant your request. The reason for this is that it's not your fault that the witnesses have not shown up. After all, you subpoenaed them to be in court! I'm not saying that you won't be able to get your case continued if you haven't subpoenaed your witnesses. It's just that if you don't, you run a greater risk of being forced to proceed without them.

If you want to subpoena a witness, the first thing you must do is to obtain a subpoena form. These forms are usually available either from the court or an office supply store. Then you will have to fill in the appropriate information on the form. This should not present any problem since these forms are usually self-explanatory, and filling them out is essentially a matter of common sense. If you need help, however, you can always ask the court clerk for advice or refer to a form book at your local law library.

After your subpoena has been prepared, the next task is to serve it on the witness. This is usually performed by a representative of the court or by a professional process server. However, it might be possible for you or one of your friends to deliver the subpoena. In any event, certain requirements generally apply regarding who can serve a subpoena, and how and when it can be served. If these requirements are not followed, the service may not be valid. Your best bet, therefore, is to check with someone from the court, or look up the rules in your state in order to be sure that you are doing it correctly.

Figures 4.3 and 4.4 are reproductions of subpoena forms that are commonly used in the New York traffic courts. Take note that Figure 4.4 is a *Subpoena Duces Tecum*, which, in addition to commanding a person to appear in court, requires him to produce any documents in his possession that may be pertinent to the case.

OBTAINING CONTINUANCES

If you find that you will not be able to attend your hearing on the designated date, don't be afraid to ask the court for a continuance. (Remember that you are flirting with trouble if you don't show up when you are supposed to.) Again, there is no guarantee that you will be successful, but as mentioned in Chapter 2, you should be able to get a continuance for a good cause and there's no harm in asking. Make sure, however, that you request it as far in advance of your hearing date as possible. In fact, I suggest that you call the court clerk as soon as you know that you will not be able to attend, even if it is weeks

Z 1147—Judicial Subpoena: Justice Court, with Witness'.
Stipulation to remain subject to Attorney's call. 9-67.

© 1967 BY JULIUS BLUMBERG, INC.,
PUBLISHER. NYC 10013

JUSTICE COURT OF THE   OF

COUNTY OF   STATE OF NEW YORK

Docket No.

Plaintiff(s)

against

JUDICIAL SUBPOENA

Defendant(s)

𝕿𝖍𝖊 𝕻𝖊𝖔𝖕𝖑𝖊 𝖔𝖋 𝖙𝖍𝖊 𝕾𝖙𝖆𝖙𝖊 𝖔𝖋 𝕹𝖊𝖜 𝖄𝖔𝖗𝖐

TO

GREETING:

    WE COMMAND YOU, *that all business and excuses being laid aside, you and each of you appear and attend before one of the Justices of this Court at*

on the   *day of*   *19*   *at*   *o'clock, in the*   *noon,*
and at any recessed or adjourned date to give testimony in this action on the part of the

    Failure to comply with this subpoena is punishable as a contempt of Court and shall make you liable to the person on whose behalf this subpoena was issued for a penalty not to exceed fifty dollars and all damages sustained by reason of your failure to comply

Dated:

The name (Clerk's—Justice's—Attorney's) must be printed beneath.

Attorney(s) for

Office and Post Office Address

FIGURE 4.3 FORMS MAY BE PURCHASED FROM JULIUS BLUMBERG, INC. NY, NY 10013, OR ANY OF ITS DEALERS. REPRODUCTION PROHIBITED.

Blumbergs Law Products

T 1149—Judicial Subpoena Duces Tecum, Justice Court, with Witness' Stipulation to remain subject to Attorney's call. 7-78.

© 1967 BY JULIUS BLUMBERG, INC., PUBLISHER. NYC 10013

JUSTICE COURT OF THE   OF
COUNTY OF   STATE OF NEW YORK

Docket No.

Plaintiff(s)

against

JUDICIAL SUBPOENA DUCES TECUM

Defendant(s)

The People of the State of New York

TO

GREETING:

WE COMMAND YOU, *that all business and excuses being laid aside, you and each of you appear and attend before one of the Justices of this Court at*

on the   day of   19   at   o'clock, in the   noon, *and at any recessed or adjourned date to give testimony in this action on the part of the*

and that you bring with you, and produce at the time and place aforesaid, a certain

now in your custody, and all other deeds, evidences and writings, which you have in your custody or power, concerning the premises.

Failure to comply with this subpoena is punishable as a contempt of Court and shall make you liable to the person on whose behalf this subpoena was issued for a penalty not to exceed fifty dollars and all damages sustained by reason of your failure to comply

Dated:

The name (Clerk's—Justice's—Attorney's) must be printed beneath.

Attorney(s) for

Office and Post Office Address

FIGURE 4.4   FORMS MAY BE PURCHASED FROM JULIUS BLUMBERG, INC. NY, NY 10013, OR ANY OF ITS DEALERS. REPRODUCTION PROHIBITED.

before your hearing. In that way, you will increase your chances of getting a continuance. Conversely, if you wait until the morning of your hearing, you will probably be turned down. Then you may be forced to attend the hearing at a great inconvenience to you.

When you ask the clerk for a continuance, ask for a new date when you know you can be fully prepared and ready to go. For example, if the clerk suggests postponing your case for two weeks, but you need six weeks, ask for it. Don't create a situation where you will be squeezed for time. The reason I say this is that if you're not prepared to proceed when the new date comes up, you may not be able to have your case continued a second time. Don't assume that you can get your case continued again and again.

You can usually obtain a continuance by simply calling or writing the court clerk. I've learned through experience, though, that calling the clerk and following up with a confirming letter is the best way of doing it. If you make a copy of your letter, you have proof that you made a request. This could come in handy if a problem arises later. Figure 4.5 is a sample letter confirming a continuance which you may wish to use as a model in composing your own.

There may be an additional advantage in obtaining a continuance; with the passage of time, the chances become greater that the state will not be able to prove its case against you. For example, by extending the time between your violation and the court hearing, records can be lost, memories can fade, witnesses can become unavailable, and so forth. I am *not* saying that you should ask for a continuance just because you think the state's case will suffer. What I *am* suggesting, however, is that if you have a legitimate reason for requesting a continuance, you should do so. It can only help.

```
To:   Court Clerk
      Name and address of Traffic Court

Re:   Your Name
      Traffic Ticket #
      Date of Offense


Dear Sir/Madam:

This letter is to confirm my recent conversation with you, in
which you postponed the hearing of my traffic case until (insert
new date).  I anticipate being ready to proceed at that time.

Thank you for your cooperation.

Very Truly Yours,



(Your signature)
```

FIGURE 4.5   CONFIRMATION OF A CONTINUANCE.

PREPARING YOUR WITNESSES

There is no doubt that the witnesses that you bring to your hearing can have a positive impact on your case. However, a witness is not going to help you very much if his testimony does not support your innocence! For example, if you were charged with disregarding a traffic signal, what do you think would happen if one of your witnesses said that the light might have been red when you passed through it? If you think this would be disastrous to your case you are probably right! Thus, in order to avoid any surprises, I suggest that you *interview* your proposed witnesses before trial. By doing this, you'll at least have a good idea of what they will say when they testify in court. Then, if you don't like what any given witness has to say, you can avoid using that person.

During your interview, you can find out what a witness knows by reviewing the facts surrounding the incident with him. If there are details that he does not recall, you can try refreshing his recollection by having him read the police report, witness statements, or other documentation you may have obtained through discovery. You might also try asking your witness to write down all he remembers about the incident. This can enhance his ability to give a detailed and persuasive account when he testifies.

Now, I'm not saying that it's good to put words into a witness' mouth. On the contrary, if that happens, that person's testimony may not sound genuine. Instead, make sure the details come from the witness' own recollection. Actually, it's a good idea to explain to your witnesses that their basic purpose is to give a truthful account of the incident. Let them know that this is essential if your case is to be decided fairly. If you urge them to be sincere, their testimony will no doubt be more believable. This concept can be illustrated by a quote made by the Greek poet, Sophocles: "Truth is always the strongest argument."

It's also essential that you mention to your witnesses that they are likely to be cross-examined by the state. Let them know that this is done mainly for the purpose of attacking their credibility. If they are aware of the importance of being truthful, however, they shouldn't have much to worry about. Indeed, if they simply tell the truth, it will be difficult for the state to make them look as though they are dishonest or unsure. In addition, you might also mention to your witnesses that they should never change their story—no matter how many times they are asked the same question by the prosecutor. Without a doubt, if they are inconsistent, their credibility will be adversely affected.

During cross-examination, your witnesses may be asked whether they discussed the case with you prior to the hearing. I've seen this question used by prosecutors as an attempt to rattle witnesses by getting them to think that they have done something wrong by discussing the case beforehand. This, however, is not so. There is nothing wrong with discussing your case with your witnesses before court! And if your witnesses know about this, they will be able to avoid being intimidated by the prosecutor.

Finally, don't forget to inform your witnesses of the date and time of your hearing, as well as the location of the court. They should also be aware of the possibility that there may be substantial waiting time due to the miscellaneous delays that often occur in court. In view of this, they should be prepared to take the entire day off from work if the need arises.

GETTING YOUR "ACT" TOGETHER

When you testify at your hearing, it is of critical importance to be *convincing*. Of course, you may be the kind of individual who has a hard time convincing others, but there are things that you can do to enhance your abilities in this regard, one of which is to make sure that you fully *prepare* your presentation in advance of your hearing. There are many ways to go about doing this, but in my opinion, the best way is to prepare a detailed written account of your story. This gives you the opportunity to read it over and add any details you may have forgotten to include. Then before your hearing, you can review it and go through a "trial run," so that everything is fresh in your mind. Think of it as your "script" for court, so to speak.

Don't fall into the trap of memorizing it, however, because that might make you sound as if your testimony has been "rehearsed." In other words, the general idea is to let it serve the purpose of refreshing your recollection. In short, be spontaneous when you testify.

Again, one of the major considerations in preparing a written account is that it will help you to remember *details.* You may not realize it, but small details (like, for example, the number of cars on the road or the time of day) are very important. One of the reasons for the importance of detail is that such testimony usually gives the impression that you have a good recollection of the incident. This can enhance your ability to be persuasive. In addition, if you know every facet of your story very well, you are less likely to make inconsistent statements when you are cross-examined by the state. Moreover, you should not underestimate the value of thorough preparation before you set foot in the courtroom. Actually, lawyers sum it up well with the saying: "A case is won in the office."

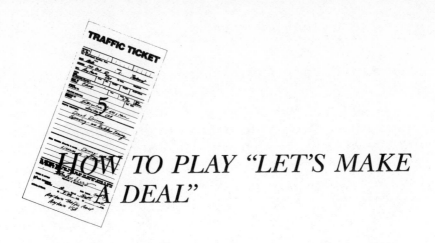

HOW TO PLAY "LET'S MAKE A DEAL"

As an alternative to trying your case, you may have the opportunity to "settle" it before trial. That is to say, you can sometimes avoid the potential consequences of a trial by negotiating for an agreed result. In many jurisdictions, this is accomplished by literally "making a deal" (plea bargaining) with the prosecutor.

Depending on your particular situation, entering into a plea bargain can sometimes make a lot of sense. As in any other important decision, however, the good and bad points should always be considered. On the plus side, a plea bargain can give you the opportunity at least to avoid partially the consequences of your traffic violations. But, on the minus side, you will be giving up your right to a hearing and the possibility of having your case dismissed in its entirety.

In order to make an intelligent decision as to whether or not to enter into a plea bargain, you should consider the following: (1) the chances of winning your case if you try it, (2) the penalties that might result if you lose, and (3) the benefits you would gain from entering into a plea bargain. In essence, these considerations boil down to the fact that you probably shouldn't agree to a plea bargain if you have a very strong case; that is, one which you are almost sure that you can win. In contrast, if you think there is a substantial likelihood that you will be found guilty, a plea bargain certainly makes a lot more sense.

If you negotiate for a plea bargain, you will normally be requested to plead guilty to one or more of the offenses you are charged with. In return, however, you can expect to have one or more of the offenses either dismissed completely, or "downgraded" to a lesser offense. Another possibility is to plead guilty to an offense in order to get a lighter sentence. To illustrate these concepts, let's take a look at four of the basic types of plea bargain agreements you're likely to encounter.

1. *Dismissal.* This type of plea bargain can come into play if you are charged with more than one offense. What happens is that one (or more) of the offenses is dismissed on the condition that you plead guilty to one (or more) of the remaining offenses. For example, let's say that you are charged with the offenses of drunk driving, driving while suspended, reckless driving, and speeding (ouch!). A typical plea bargain in a case like this might consist of your promise to plead guilty to drunk driving and driving while suspended, in return for the dismissal of the reckless driving and speeding charges.

2. *Merger.* This type of plea bargain occurs when there are two similar offenses that are, in effect, "merged" (consolidated) into one offense. So instead of facing charges on two offenses, you would simply plead guilty to one of them. For example, let's say that you are charged with the offenses of speeding and careless driving. In a case like this, the careless driving would merge with speeding, so that only the speeding offense would remain. You should understand that the lesser included offense (careless driving) usually merges with the greater offense (speeding). In other words, the act of careless driving is essentially included in the act of speeding and can, so to speak, be *absorbed* into the speeding offense. (If you reverse the situ-

ation, you can see that speeding is not *necessarily* included in careless driving.)

3. *Downgrading.* In this type of plea bargain, the original offense you are charged with is reduced (downgraded) to a less serious offense, on the condition that you plead guilty to the lesser offense. For example, if you were charged with reckless driving, you might be able to have the charge reduced to careless driving. Or, if you were charged with racing on the highway, you might have that charge downgraded to a simple speeding ticket.

4. *Reduced Sentence.* In this type of plea bargain, you are required to plead guilty to the offense you are charged with in return for a lighter sentence than you would normally expect to get. For example, suppose that you are charged with the offense of driving while suspended, which carries a possible jail sentence. If the prosecutor assured you that you would receive only a fine, you might elect to plead guilty and eliminate any risk of going to jail.

Keep in mind that there is a lot of strategy involved in the plea bargaining process. Above all, your ability to demonstrate that you have a winning case is critical. In other words, let the prosecutor know that you have prepared your case thoroughly and you are ready to go to trial. Also let him know that you believe that you have a valid defense. If you do this, he may start to wonder about *his* ability to win the case. In short, if he believes that you might win, he will probably be willing to compromise. Don't forget, even though you may be dying to make a deal, it may not be a good idea to let it show in your attitude. I think this is summed up very well by something the American author, Elbert Hubbard, once said: "It is the weak man who urges compromise—never the strong man."

Here's another thing you should consider. Let's say that you want to plea bargain your case, because you have no intention of trying it. Even so, it is nonetheless important to be prepared to proceed with trial. Don't forget that a plea bargain may not be available, and even if one is offered to you, it may not be to your liking. Also, as I mentioned before, you will be in a stronger bargaining position if you have prepared your case.

I should also mention that there may be a few stumbling blocks to your being able to arrange a plea bargain. First of all, plea bargaining may not be available if the practice is not followed in your locale. Also, judges generally have the authority to refuse a plea bargain for just about any reason. So even if you have negotiated one with the prosecutor, the judge may not be receptive to the idea. The judges I've run across, however, have almost invariably approved plea bargains. What I'm really saying is that if the prosecutor recommends a settlement, most judges would not want to engage in a potentially lengthy trial if they don't have to. Finally, the availability of a plea bargain may also depend on whether the police officers involved in the case are in favor of the idea. In my experience, I've found that most prosecutors like to first speak with the officer before they agree to a plea bargain. So the lesson to be learned here is that if you give the officer a hard time when he stops you, he may tell the prosecutor not to give you a break. Conversely, if you are polite and cooperative, he may even go out of his way to see that you are not dealt with too harshly. Moreover, it's wise to make every effort to be cooperative with the police. It can pay big dividends!

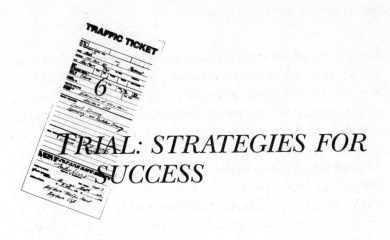

TRIAL: STRATEGIES FOR SUCCESS

GENERAL SEQUENCE OF EVENTS

Your traffic court no doubt has a standard procedure that it more or less follows when it conducts its hearings. If you have a basic understanding of that procedure, it can be a big plus. Essentially, if you know what's coming up next at trial, you can plan your strategy much more efficiently.

As I mentioned before, this book is geared toward the majority of jurisdictions in which traffic hearings are treated basically as formal trials in a courtroom. With this in mind, the following list was created to illustrate the sequence of events that is typically followed at most traffic hearings.

1. You enter your plea of not guilty.
2. The state's witness(es) testify against you (direct testimony).
3. You have the opportunity to question each of the state's witnesses (cross-examination by the defense).
4. The state has the opportunity to obtain additional testimony from its witnesses (redirect testimony by the state).
5. The state rests its case.
6. You and your witnesses (if any) testify one by one (direct testimony).

7. The state has the opportunity to question you and your witnesses (cross-examination by the state).
8. You and your witnesses have the opportunity to supply additional testimony (redirect testimony by the defense).
9. You give your summation.
10. The prosecutor gives his summation on behalf of the state.
11. The judge (or jury) renders a verdict.
12. If you are found guilty, an appropriate sentence is then imposed. Or, if you are found not guilty, your case is dismissed.

Keep in mind that this list should serve as a general outline only, since your particular hearing may not conform in all respects. In addition, the list does not include all of the optional strategies (such as objections, motions, or statements regarding sentencing) that you may want to use at your trial.

CROSS-EXAMINING THE OPPOSITION

Needless to say, your primary objective in cross-examining a witness for the state is to discredit that individual's testimony. Essentially, this can be done by showing that: (1) the witness has made inconsistent statements, and/or (2) the witness did not have the opportunity to observe the offense, and/or (3) the observation was faulty.

INCONSISTENT STATEMENTS

Quite frequently, an opposing (adverse) witness makes a statement while testifying at trial that is inconsistent with something the witness has already said or wrote. Now, if you can expose such an inconsistency, you can usually shed some degree of uncertainty on that witness' statements.

For example, imagine that you are on trial for reckless driving, and the police officer, whom we shall call Officer Law, has testified during direct examination that your vehicle was traveling at approximately sixty-five miles per hour. But assume that during your cross-examination, Officer Law admitted that you might have actually been traveling at a speed between fifty and fifty-five miles an hour.

Clearly, there is an inconsistency in Officer Law's statements regarding his estimate of your speed. So by confronting him with his statements, this inconsistency can be exposed. Now take a look at the following illustration, that shows one way this could be accomplished through cross-examination.

> *You:* Officer, isn't it true that a few minutes ago during your direct testimony, you estimated that the speed of my vehicle was sixty-five miles per hour?
>
> *Officer Law:* Yes.
>
> *You:* Now do you remember also telling me during my cross-examination that I could have been going between fifty and fifty-five miles per hour?
>
> *Officer Law:* *Yes.*
>
> *You:* Isn't it true then, that you're really not sure how fast I was going?
>
> *Officer Law:* Well, I'm not exactly sure.

Here you can see that by confronting Officer Law with his conflicting statements, you are in effect revealing the fact that he is not really sure how fast you were traveling. As a result, his testimony, not only on this particular point, but in general, is somewhat less believable.

The next sample illustration shows how you might go about exposing an inconsistency where one of the inconsistent statements is *written* in his police report.

> *You:* Officer, do you remember preparing a police report regarding the offense I'm charged with?

> *Officer Law:* Yes I do.
>
> *You:* Is this the police report that you prepared? (Note: at this point, you would normally hand the officer a copy of the police report and let him examine it.)
>
> *Officer Law:* Yes.
>
> *You:* Isn't it true that you wrote on the police report that you estimated the speed of my vehicle to be sixty-five miles per hour?
>
> *Officer Law:* Yes.
>
> *You:* And isn't it also true that just a moment ago, you testified under oath that I was going fifty to fifty-five miles per hour?
>
> *Officer Law:* Yes.

The comment should be made that, although unlikely, it's possible that a witness may deny having made a statement in order to cover up an inconsistency. If this occurs, however, you may be able to expose the statement by having the applicable portion of the recorded transcript read back in open court (assuming that your court makes a record of its proceedings). But even if that is not possible, I wouldn't worry about it if I were you because it's likely that the judge will have heard the inconsistent statement anyway. Besides this, the witness' attempted cover-up will probably damage his credibility since he may appear to be devious in hiding the truth.

FAILURE TO OBSERVE

Another way to win your case is by showing that no one actually saw you commit the offense you are charged with. This is possible since in most cases, the state needs to produce an eyewitness in order to convict you of a moving traffic violation. So even though you may *think* that the state's witness observed the incident that led to your traffic ticket, you should not assume this. Rather, you should make it a point during your cross-examination to find out *exactly* what each witness saw.

For example, imagine that you are involved in a minor accident with another driver (Mr. Unfriendly). Assume that when the police officer (Officer Law) came to the scene five minutes later, Mr. Unfriendly told him that you ran the stop sign. Consequently, you were given a traffic ticket. The following sample illustration shows how you might cross-examine Officer Law at trial in order to expose his failure to observe the incident.

> *You:* Officer, at the time I supposedly ran the stop sign at Main and Oak Street, where were you?
>
> *Officer Law:* I was driving in my patrol car on the other side of town.
>
> *You:* So then you did not personally see me go through the stop sign without stopping?
>
> *Officer Law:* No.
>
> *You:* Then why did you write me a ticket for that offense?
>
> *Officer Law:* Because Mr. Unfriendly told me that you ran the stop sign.
>
> *You:* Is he in court today to testify against me?
>
> *Officer Law:* No.

Now if you were actually involved in this situation, it is apparent that the state would not have a case against you. First of all, Officer Law did not see anything. Second, he can't testify as to something Mr. Unfriendly told him because it would be inadmissible hearsay evidence. (Note: hearsay evidence is discussed in Chapter 7.)

The above illustration is also a good example of something that you will learn in Chapter 9. That is, if it becomes apparent that the state does not have a case, you can sometimes have your charges dismissed *immediately*. This can be done by making a motion to dismiss for failure to prove a prima facie case.

FAULTY OBSERVATION

It is also very common to run across a situation in which a witness' perception of an incident was faulty for one reason or another. Example: Perhaps a police officer's view was unclear because it was dark outside. Or, maybe his attention was distracted momentarily, which caused him to look in another direction.

Clearly, it can be a tremendous advantage if you can reveal a witness' faulty observation at trial. To illustrate, consider a hypothetical situation. Imagine that you have been charged with disregarding a stop sign. Also, assume that the police officer who ticketed you (Officer Law) did not have a clear observation of the incident because his view was blocked. The following sample cross-examination shows how you might question Officer Law in order to expose his faulty observation:

You:	Officer, at the time I allegedly ran the stop sign at the intersection of Main and Oak Street, where were you?
Officer Law:	I was sitting in my patrol car.
You:	Please tell me where your vehicle was located at that time.
Officer Law:	I was parked on the right side of Oak Street, facing north, approximately fifty yards south of the intersection with Main.
You:	From where you were parked, did you have a clear line of sight to the stop sign that you say I disregarded?
Officer Law:	Yes.
You:	Do you recall what the weather conditions were at the time?
Officer Law:	Clear and dry.
You:	Were there any vehicles parked in front of your patrol car?
Officer Law:	No.
You:	When did you first observe my car?
Officer Law:	I first saw you as you passed my vehicle on the left side, going north on Oak Street.

> *You:* What time of day was it?
> *Officer Law:* About 2:00 P.M.
> *You:* Did you notice if there were any vehicles in front of my car waiting at the stop sign?
> *Officer Law:* I believe there was one.
> *You:* Do you recall if there were any vehicles following my car when I reached the intersection with Main Street?
> *Officer Law:* Yes, I think there were two, maybe three.
> *You:* What type of vehicles were they?
> *Officer Law:* I think there were two cars and a pickup truck.
> *You:* Did you see my car go past the stop sign and cross Main Street without stopping?
> *Officer Law:* Yes.
> *You:* Did you notice if my brake lights were on when I reached the stop sign?
> *Officer Law:* I didn't see them go on.
> *You:* Isn't it a fact that you did not see them go on because there were three vehicles in back of mine blocking your view?
> *Officer Law:* That's true.
> *You:* And isn't it also true that since you could not see my brake lights, you really don't know whether they were on or not?
> *Officer Law:* I'm not sure.
> *You:* Thank you officer, that's all.

Now can you see that cross-examination can be very effective in exposing a witness' faulty observation? In this illustration, Officer Law's statement that you failed to stop became doubtful as soon as it was revealed that he didn't even see your brake lights. Also, when he admitted that there were three vehicles following yours, it suggested that he might have had difficulty seeing your car, if indeed he saw it at all!

Also notice that in one answer, Officer Law is being evasive when he states that he did not *see* the parking lights go on. True, he didn't see the lights go on, but he failed to mention the reason *why* he didn't see them go on. That is, because his view was blocked! See how this extra bit of information sheds a completely different light on the situation? Since witnesses sometimes omit things that are essential to a full understanding of the situation, it is up to you to extract this information through your cross-examination. I think the point here can be summed up by something that Robert Lewis Stevenson, the Scottish novelist, once said: "The cruelest lies are often told in silence."

There are a couple of additional points you should consider. For starters, notice that the cross-examination was stopped after Officer Law admitted that he was not sure whether the brake lights were on. This was done for a reason. Suppose that an additional question was asked such as: "If you did not see my brake lights, why do you think that I failed to stop?" Do you see how this might give Officer Law an opportunity to bring up additional reasons to support his assertion that you did not stop? Put it this way: once you get a favorable response and make your point, you should either go on to the next point, or end your cross-examination.

In addition, don't forget that a witness' observation can be adversely affected by weather conditions such as fog, rain, snow, or darkness. That is why the illustration contained questions that covered these points. Again, it is up to you to find out if anything interfered with the witness' view of the occurrence.

ADDITIONAL TIPS

The number of witnesses the state presents at trial will of course depend on the circumstances in any given case. Besides the investigating police officer, there may be additional witnesses such as pedestrians, passengers, or other drivers, who may have knowledge of the incident. In view of this, it's helpful to find out who the state intends to call as witnesses by requesting this information through discovery prior to your hearing. By doing this, you can plan your cross-examination in advance.

If you prepare a list of questions to ask the state's witnesses (or even an outline of the general areas you want to cover), you will undoubtedly be more effective when you cross-examine them than if you go in "cold." The technique I use is to bring an outline covering the general areas of inquiry I plan to explore during my cross-examination. Then, as each witness testifies during direct, I make it a point to supplement my outline with any additional points the witnesses may bring up. Let me emphasize that it's difficult to think of everything you want to ask a witness in court without at least an outline. You will probably be a little nervous, and as a result, you might forget to ask some important questions. So be smart and prepare in advance.

It's generally a good idea to control the witness you are cross-examining so that he doesn't have the opportunity to volunteer information that can be damaging to your case. (When you give them the chance, witnesses like to do this sort of thing.) Accordingly, you should attempt to phrase your questions so that the witness is limited to a short answer. If you will notice, most of the questions in the sample illustration shown earlier in this chapter are phrased in such a manner.

Another point to consider is that it's usually not a good idea to give the witness an opportunity to supply information if he has left it out during his direct testimony. For example, if you are prosecuted for reckless driving, it is typical for the police officer to testify as to the way in which you operated your vehicle at the time of the incident. The police officer, however, may *omit* information that would hurt your case—such as comments that you were weaving, or that you ran up a curb. On cross-examination then, it may not be a good idea for you to ask questions such as: "Did you see me weaving?," or, "Did you see me run up a curb?" It should be apparent that asking questions such as these will give the officer a good opportunity to fill in the missing information that he forgot to include.

Also, make sure you project a pleasant attitude during cross-examination. You probably have seen many television shows where a witness was grilled relentlessly by a lawyer whose attitude was rude or sarcastic. In my view, this type of attitude will not get you very far. As the saying goes, "You can catch more flies with honey than with vinegar." Also, if you are courteous and friendly to the witnesses you cross-examine, they are much more apt to be cooperative and responsive to your questions. Another advantage is that you will make a better impression on the judge.

You should also consider the fact that it's not always necessary or even desirable to cross-examine a witness. When a witness' direct testimony has been confusing or vague (or if the witness sounds about as believable as someone insisting that robbing banks is a lawful enterprise), I don't bother to cross-examine. Indeed, it might only serve to give the witness the opportunity to improve on what was said.

PRESENTING YOUR OWN TESTIMONY

When you testify in court, you are engaging in the art of persuasion. Simply put, what you are trying to do is to get the judge to see things your way. So in order to improve your persuasiveness, I suggest that you observe the following basic guidelines:

1. Give a complete and detailed account of your version of the facts. The importance of this guideline can be appreciated by considering the following hypothetical example. Imagine that you have been charged with unlawfully passing a stopped school bus. At trial, assume the police officer testifies that the bus had its lights flashing and there were children getting off the bus when you passed it. But you know that he is mistaken and, of course, want to convince the court to believe your story.

The following two versions are provided as illustrations of how you might go about presenting your testimony at trial. One of the versions is obviously much more persuasive than the other.

Version A

When I approached the school bus, I didn't notice any flashing lights or see any children, so I didn't stop my car.

Version B

As I was driving along Main Street, I noticed that I was headed toward a yellow school bus parked to my left on the shoulder of the road. When I first noticed it, I was approximately two blocks away. At that point, its lights were flashing. I then slowed my car down to about twenty miles an hour in anticipation of stopping. But, before I got to the bus, I distinctly remember that its flashing lights went off. Of course, I still made it a point to look and see if any children were getting on or off, but I didn't see any, so I proceeded to drive past the bus.

Now, if you were the judge, which version would you believe? Obviously, Version B is much better. It's *detailed*, and it gives a *complete* account of the incident. As a result, it's quite believable. In contrast, Version A sounds like something that a person who was actually guilty of the offense would say. It lacks substance and gives one the impression that it is "fabricated."

If you think about it, you should realize that it's not easy for someone to describe an incident in any detail if he or she is simply "making it up." Of course, the judge is aware of this as well. It follows, then, if you can include many of the details about an incident, the judge is more apt to believe that you are telling the truth.

2. Be positive—don't be vague or uncertain. It's always a good idea to be positive when you testify in court. This makes sense because a positive attitude conveys the message that *you* believe in what you are saying! In fact, if you feel emotional about certain things, I think it's a good idea to let some of it show. Your emotion shows that you believe in the righteousness of your cause. Needless to say, don't go overboard on your emotional display, since then you could do more harm than good.

3. Don't change your story or make inconsistent statements. As we discussed previously in this chapter, a person's credibility can be damaged if he or she makes inconsistent statements. Keep this in mind when you testify. Suffice it to say that if you contradict yourself, you can usually be confident that the prosecutor will make the most of it.

4. Be as accurate as possible—don't exaggerate. In order to illustrate this concept, let's go back to Version B in the second guideline above. Refer to the portion of testimony where it is stated: "I then slowed my car down to about twenty miles per hour in anticipation of stopping." Now, suppose that the statement was: "I then slowed my car down to about *five* miles per hour in anticipation of stopping." Here, the point is that most people would not slow down to a speed of five miles per hour when they were two blocks away from a school bus. In other words, twenty miles per hour sounds okay, but five miles per hour sounds very exaggerated. It is simply much too slow to be realistic. Moreover, if you make a ridiculous or exaggerated statement, you run the risk of straining the judge's credulity. I should also mention that if you exaggerate, even on one point, the judge may be led to believe that everything you say is an exaggeration. That would indeed be unfortunate.

EXAMINING YOUR OWN WITNESSES

When you call your witnesses to testify, they will be questioned with regard to what they know about the incident. This is referred to as direct examination. Depending on the policy followed in your traffic court, the judge might conduct the examination. However, it is possible that you yourself may get the chance to question your witnesses. Now you might be asking, "is it better to let the judge conduct the direct examination, or should I do it myself?" Well, it depends. Assuming that you do a competent job, it can be advantageous to do it yourself. This is mainly because your witness may omit some important information if he is questioned by the judge. On the other hand, if you ask the questions, you can make sure that your witness covers all of the important points that you want the judge to hear.

Whereas the basic purpose of cross-examination is to tear down an opposing witness' credibility, direct examination is designed to do just the opposite—that is, to build the credibility of your own witness. Therefore, the questioning technique you should use in conducting a direct examination is altogether different from that used in cross-examination. To illustrate, consider a hypothetical example. Suppose that Officer Law gave you a speeding ticket for going sixty-five miles per hour in a fifty-five-mile-per-hour zone. Assume you are contesting the ticket because you're sure that you were traveling between fifty and fifty-five miles per hour. Let's also say that your passenger at the time, who we shall call Frank Friendly, has agreed to help you by testifying for you in court. Now, your direct examination might go something like this:

You:	What's your name?
Friendly:	Frank Friendly.
You:	Where do you live?
Friendly:	10 Oak Street, Lindenwold, N.J.
You:	What were you doing on December 5th between the hours of 3:P.M. and 3:30P.M.?
Friendly:	I was a passenger in your car.
You:	Who was driving?
Friendly:	You were.
You:	Do you recall where we were going?
Friendly:	Shopping at the Deptford Mall.
You:	Do you remember what happened on Rt. 42?
Friendly:	Yes—we were pulled over by Officer Law. I guess it was about a minute or two after we entered onto Route 42. He then issued you a ticket for speeding on Route 42.
You:	Do you know what our speed was between the time we got onto Route 42 and the time that we were pulled over?
Friendly:	Yes I do.
You:	How do you know?
Friendly:	Because I was looking at your speedometer. Whenever I ride in someone else's car, I have a habit of checking their speed by continually looking over at the speedometer.
You:	How fast were we going according to my speedometer?
Friendly:	Between fifty and fifty-five miles per hour.
You:	Was there ever a time when you saw my speed rise above fifty-five?
Friendly:	Not while I was in the car.

The main point you should learn from this illustration is that *it's important to question your witness in such a way that you find out what he bases his statements on.* For example, it was important to bring out the point that Frank Friendly's estimate of speed was based on his checking the car's speedometer. If this bit of information had not been revealed, do you think his testimony would be as believable? I don't. In essence, then, if your witness gives the specific reasons that support his statements, his testimony will no doubt be given more weight than testimony of others not so supported. This will be more helpful to you.

ADDITIONAL TIPS

If you don't want to examine your witnesses, that's okay. You may be more comfortable with simply letting the judge do it. However, if you want to give it a try, you should ask the judge for permission to do so. It's possible that he may deny your request, but you have nothing to lose by asking.

You might also be wondering about the order in which your witnesses should testify. There is no hard and fast rule in this regard. Just try to have them testify in a logical order. When I try a case, I usually have my client (the defendant) testify *before* his supporting witnesses. I do this mainly because the other witnesses I have brought to testify will have their memories refreshed after they hear what my client has to say.

I should also make the comment that if you have a witness who doesn't understand the English language well enough to testify, it may be necessary for you to hire an interpreter to translate in court. If you don't know where to look for one, ask the court clerk, who deals with this problem from time to time. You might check to see if your witness has any relatives or friends who will volunteer to act in this capacity.

In summary, keep in mind that the suggestions relating to how you can enhance your credibility that were covered in the last section are equally applicable to your witnesses when they testify. Accordingly, it's a good idea to acquaint them with those concepts. Then they will no doubt make better witnesses.

GIVING YOUR SUMMATION

If you've ever wanted to be an actor or actress, this is the opportunity you've been waiting for! Of course, I'm just kidding when I say this, but actually, a summation, or closing argument, involves a little bit of acting. In other words, it gives you the chance to give a little speech in your own behalf and emphasize the reasons why your case should be dismissed.

To illustrate this, let's take a look at a hypothetical situation that will serve as a background for the sample summation that follows. Imagine that you have been charged with failure to yield to a pedestrian at a cross-walk. Assume that at trial, the state's only witness, Officer Law, testified that he observed your vehicle pass through the crosswalk without yielding to the pedestrian, Mr. Walker, who was about to cross the street. Your position is that you did not have enough time to yield because Mr. Walker suddenly ran out from the sidewalk just as you reached the crosswalk. Let's also say that during your cross-examination of Officer Law, he admitted that he didn't see your car until it was halfway past the crosswalk.

You should consider that the main purpose of the following sample summation is to persuade the judge that your conduct—when compared with the section of the law that describes the offense—was simply not illegal. Please note that for purposes of illustration, the Pennsylvania statute that deals with a pedestrian's right-of-way has been referred to in the sample summation. For your reference, it has been reproduced in Figure 6.1.

Sample Summation

Your Honor, I know that the section of the law I am charged under requires a motorist to yield to pedestrians crossing the street. However, the law specifically prohibits a pedestrian from leaving a curb

---

§ **3542.** **Right-of-way of pedestrians in crosswalks**

(a) **General rule.**—When traffic-control signals are not in place or not in operation, the driver of a vehicle shall yield the right-of-way to a pedestrian crossing the roadway within any marked crosswalk or within any unmarked crosswalk at an intersection.

(b) **Exercise of care by pedestrian.**—No pedestrian shall suddenly leave a curb or other place of safety and walk or run into the path of a vehicle which is so close as to constitute a hazard.

(c) **Limitation on vehicles passing.**—Whenever any vehicle is stopped at any crosswalk at an intersection or at any marked crosswalk to permit a pedestrian to cross the roadway, the driver of any other vehicle approaching from the rear shall not overtake and pass the stopped vehicle.

(d) **Application of section.**—Subsection (a) does not apply under the conditions stated in section 3543(b) (relating to pedestrians crossing at other than crosswalks).

FIGURE 6.1 PURDON'S PENNSYLVANIA STATUTES ANNOTATED

and running into the path of a vehicle so as to create a hazard. In my case, Mr. Walker had a legal duty to stay out of my way since he should have known that I didn't have enough time to stop. I'll admit that Officer Law testified that he observed my car proceed through the crosswalk without allowing Mr. Walker to cross the street. But Officer Law candidly admitted during cross-examination that I was already half past the crosswalk when he first saw my car. That means it was obviously too late for him to see Mr. Walker dart out from the curb! In view of this, it's clear that the state has not proven its case. Accordingly, the charge should be dismissed.

Now, let's briefly analyze this summation. As you can see, the basic idea that was brought out was that there was simply no violation of the law. In other words, it's not illegal to fail to yield if a pedestrian acts in a way that makes it impossible to yield.

Another idea that was brought out was that Officer Law's observation was faulty. That is to say that Mr. Walker had *already* darted out from the curb before Officer Law even took notice of the incident. Hence, he didn't really know if an offense was committed or not.

Now do you think that a judge would find you guilty if this were an actual case? I certainly don't. (At least he shouldn't.) Again, remember that all it takes to win is to introduce some doubt in your case.

ADDITIONAL TIPS

Bear in mind that your summation does not have to be structured exactly the same as the above illustration. For example, you might want to save your discussion of the law till the end. Or, you may not want to comment on the testimony from the state's witnesses if you don't think it's worthwhile. In other words, there is no set formula regarding the structure of your summation. You can be creative and basically say things in your own words. The main thing to remember, though, is to make your summation *logical*. I say this because logic tends to be the most powerful form of persuasion. Saint Exupery, the French writer, put it this way: "Anything can be demonstrated by logic."

Also, your summation need not be long and drawn out to be effective. It's okay if you simply make your point and stop at that. In fact, a lot of unimportant verbiage can "dilute" the impact of the main issue in the case. Besides, I don't think that judges appreciate lengthy closing arguments, especially when they have a large volume of cases to deal with and can't afford to waste any time.

Here's another tip. Always make an effort to be *accurate* if you comment on a witness' testimony. If you mistake something a witness said during trial, you run the risk of looking like a liar. I'm not saying that you're expected to remember what a witness says verbatim. But if a witness said, for example, that the light was red and you say during summation that he or she said it was green, this could be a problem. Even though such a misstatement might be an innocent mistake, the judge may think that it was made intentionally.

Let me also mention that it's a good idea to prepare an outline of your summation *before* your hearing. By doing this, you will have the time to analyze carefully the section you are charged under and then compare it with the facts in your case. In addition, if you hear a witness make a statement that you want to refer to in your summation, remember to jot it down on your outline. This way, you won't forget it, and you will be less likely to misstate what the witness said.

Finally, you should consider the fact that you don't have to give a summation if you don't want to. If you want my opinion, though, I look at it as being the last opportunity to stress the positive aspects of a case. This is why I almost always give a summation. In fact, I'm sure that in more than a few borderline cases that I've tried, my summation was the key to my success.

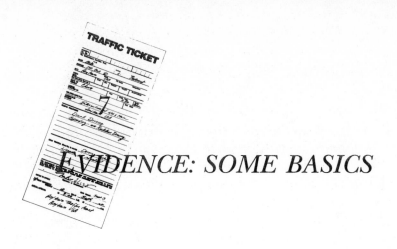

EVIDENCE: SOME BASICS

Evidence can be defined simply as information that demonstrates the truth or falsehood of the point in issue. It can consist of verbal testimony from a witness (testimonial evidence), or in the form of an exhibit, such as a photograph or diagram (demonstrative evidence). Of course, not all of the information that is submitted at trial is acceptable as evidence. If the judge decides that something is objectionable—for any one of a variety of reasons—he has the power to exclude it and declare it to be inadmissible. Conversely, if he decides that the information submitted is not objectionable, he should admit it into evidence.

Although you will most likely be going into court without much knowledge on the subject of evidence, there are a couple of reasons why you shouldn't be intimidated by this. First of all, the formal rules of evidence are often relaxed in traffic court. This makes it easier to have evidence admitted at trial. The other reason is that you can, and should, depend on the judge to help you whenever you need it. (After all, one of the judge's main functions is to protect your rights.) For example, if you ask a leading question (See Chapter 8) and the prosecutor objects to it, the judge can guide you on how to rephrase it. In other words, the judge can usually tell you what you must do in order to get your evidence admitted.

However, despite the fact that the rules of evidence may be relaxed somewhat, they should still apply, at least to some degree, at your traffic hearing. In view of this, it makes sense to have at least a basic understanding of a few of the fundamental concepts. These are explored in the next three sections.

RELEVANCE

In order for evidence to be admissible at trial, one of the basic requirements is that it must be relevant. Simply put, the evidence that you want to have admitted must tend to *prove* one of the issues that relates to the case. Let me illustrate this concept by analyzing a hypothetical example. Imagine that you are charged with careless driving. Assume that in order to prove its case, the state has Officer Law testify that you swerved your car over the center line into the stream of oncoming cars. Now, do you think that such testimony is relevant? If you said yes, you're right. It's relevant because it obviously tends to prove that you were driving carelessly. On the other hand, if Officer Law had testified that you were convicted of a speeding offense last year, for example, it would not be relevant. Why? Because being convicted of a speeding ticket last year clearly has nothing to do with your present careless driving offense.

HEARSAY

For starters, let's define what hearsay is. It is (1) a statement, (2) which was *not* made by the witness who is testfying, and (3) which is being offered to prove the truth of the matter asserted. Now I know this sounds complicated, but it's really not. Just think of it as a rule that requires that a witness must testify as to what he or she saw or heard, as opposed to what someone else saw or heard. While some exceptions apply, hearsay evidence is generally inadmissable in court.

To illustrate this concept, let's look at a hypothetical situation. Imagine that you were charged with leaving the scene of an accident. Assume that at trial, the police officer, whom we will call Officer Incourt, testified that *another* police officer, whom we will call Officer Outacourt, told him that you fled from the accident scene. Now, do you see why this is hearsay? Obviously, it is because: (1) the statement being offered into evidence was made by Officer Outacourt—it was not made by Officer Incourt, who is the one testifying and (2) the statement is being offered to prove the truth of the matter asserted, i.e., that you fled from the accident scene.

At this point, I should mention one of the exceptions to the hearsay rule that has particular application in many traffic cases. That is, a police officer is generally permitted to testify as to what a motorist says *if* the statement was an admission against the motorist's own interest. In other words, if you make any *incriminating statements* to a police officer, these can usually be used as evidence against you in court. For example, if you said "I had eight drinks," or "I was going 70 mph," the officer could probably testify that you made such statements.

The point I'm making here is that when you are stopped you are not *required* to say anything that is incriminating. If a police officer asks you a question, and you think that by answering it, you will be supplying him with damaging information, you can refuse to answer. Of course, I'm not saying that you should be uncooperative, but again, you certainly have the option to politely say something like "I'm sorry, but I'd rather not answer that question."

EXHIBITS

If you plan to use an exhibit such as a photograph or sketch, be prepared to meet some basic requirements so that the judge will admit it into evidence. In legal terminology this is called "laying a foundation" for an exhibit. Simply put, you should be able to (1) identify what your exhibit is supposed to represent, and (2) show that it's an accurate representation. The court will essentially want to know that your exhibit is a fair and accurate reproduction of what it's being offered to show. So be prepared for the judge or prosecutor to ask questions along the following lines: (1) who is responsible for creating the exhibit, for example, who took the photographs or drew the diagram, (2) when it was created, (3) what it's supposed to show, and (4) whether the portrayal is the same as it existed at the time of the incident.

As mentioned previously, the judge makes the determination whether evidence should be admitted or not. Thus, if he thinks that your exhibit is irrelevant, or that it is not a fair representation of what it is meant to show, he can disallow it. However, as a general rule of thumb, if your exhibit helps the judge to obtain a better understanding of the subject matter, there is a good chance that he will admit it into evidence.

In many cases, it is necessary to go through a certain procedure in order to get an exhibit admitted into evidence. Accordingly, the following outline has been provided to give you an idea of how you might go about doing this.

1. Tell the judge that you would like to introduce your exhibit into evidence, and ask that it be marked for identification. (Note: you would normally do this during your direct testimony, just prior to the time when your exhibit would logically fit into your presentation.)

2. Answer any questions asked by the judge or prosecutor having to do with the identification and/or accuracy of the exhibit.
3. Ask the judge to admit your exhibit into evidence.

It may also be possible for you to have your exhibits admitted into evidence *without* the necessity of going through the procedure outlined above. For example, if informality prevails in your particular court, the judge might take a look at your exhibit and accept it without any questions. Or, the prosecutor (if there is one) might simply "stipulate" (agree) to its admission. Fortunately, prosecutors are often happy to cooperate in this regard because a stipulation is easier and less time-consuming than going through the "formal" procedure.

When I am in traffic court, I usually try to show the prosecutor any exhibits I plan to introduce *before* the court session begins. This at least gives me the chance to explore the possibility of getting a stipulation. Actually, I've found that prosecutors are less likely to stipulate to the admission of an exhibit in the midst of a trial if they have not seen the exhibit beforehand.

Here's something else to keep in mind. Don't be afraid to use a little imagination in the courtroom. For example, suppose that you are in court with a sketch you drew at home, but the judge does not want to admit it because he thinks it is inaccurate. What would you do in this case? Well, my suggestion would be to see if the judge will let you draw your sketch on a blackboard or a sheet of paper in court. My point here can be best expressed by making an analogy. Just because you hit a roadblock on the way to your destination, you may not have to turn around and go home. Perhaps you can take a detour that will get you there just as well.

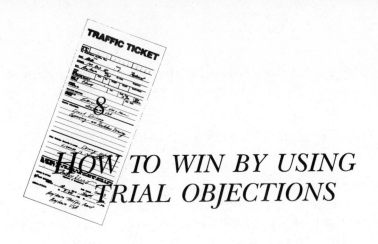

8
HOW TO WIN BY USING TRIAL OBJECTIONS

In essence, making an objection is simply a way to voice your disagreement with some improper statement or action by the state. For your purposes, objections could come in handy in the following situations: (1) when the prosecutor asks an improper question during direct or cross-examination, (2) when the prosecutor attempts to introduce an exhibit without an adequate foundation, (3) when an opposing witness' testimony contains inadmissible evidence, or (4) when an opposing witness attempts to introduce an exhibit without an adequate foundation. Keep in mind that an objection is addressed to the judge, who then decides whether it has merit or not. In other words, he can either "sustain" or "overrule" the objection.

As you might imagine, objections can be made for a variety of reasons. But for the most part, you should find them useful for the following purposes: (1) to block (or to have stricken) the testimony of the state's witnesses, or (2), to block exhibits that the state wants to have admitted into evidence.

Understand that there are so many potential reasons why objections can be made, even an attempt to discuss them all would be extremely confusing to you. Therefore, I think you will be better served by limiting our discussions to the categories that should be the most helpful to you.

OBJECTIONS REGARDING THE SUBSTANCE OF THE EVIDENCE

As discussed in the previous chapter, evidence is likely to be inadmissible if it's irrelevant or hearsay. Thus, if you suspect that the evidence that was given (or is about to be given) by an adversary witness will be inadmissible for either of those reasons, you can (and should) object to it. Assuming that the judge sustains your objection, there are a couple of results that can follow. One is that the evidence will be "stricken from the record." This occurs when the objectionable evidence has already been admitted, such as when the witness has already spoken. The other result is that the evidence is blocked. An example of this is when the witness is *prevented* from giving an answer to an objectionable question.

To give you an example of an objection that is based on hearsay, consider a hypothetical situation. Imagine that you are being prosecuted for driving under the influence. Assume that the officer who is testifying for the state, Officer Incourt, was told by another policeman, Officer Outacourt, that you were driving erratically. Also assume that during trial, the prosecutor asks Officer Incourt the following question: "Officer Incourt, did Officer Outacourt tell you that the defendant was driving erratically? Now, before Officer Incourt gives his answer, you could make the following objection: "Your Honor, I object. This question calls for Officer Incourt to give an answer that would be hearsay." At that point, the judge would probably sustain your objection and tell Officer Incourt not to answer the question.

Of course, if Officer Incourt has already answered the question, you would be unable to block his testimony. However, you could still object by saying something like:

"Your honor, Officer Incourt's answer is inadmissible because it is hearsay." Then, if your objection was sustained, the judge would typically make a statement to the effect that the evidence should be stricken from the record.

Again, you should fully understand the reason for this objection. If Officer Incourt saw you drive erratically, he could have certainly testified to it. But that was not the case. It was Officer Outacourt who *told* him that you were driving erratically—and that, my friends, is hearsay.

OBJECTIONS REGARDING THE FORM OF THE QUESTION

Even if the prosecutor asks a question that does not call for inadmissible evidence, you can still raise an objection if the *question itself* is improper. The following is a sampling of a few of the most common types of questions that are objectionable.

1. Leading Questions. When the prosecutor asks a question that is overly suggestive of the answer he wants from his witness, it is usually considered to be objectionable. As you might guess, a witness should not be given any hints at the answer desired. For example, suppose that you are being prosecuted for going through a red light. Assume that at trial, the prosecutor asks his witness, Officer Law, the following question: "Officer, I presume that you saw the defendant go through a red light?" In this example, most judges would probably consider this question to be leading because it obviously suggests the answer that the prosecutor wants to hear. In contrast to this, consider a question such as: "Officer Law, what, if anything, did you see the defendant do?" Now, this question would be acceptable because it is phrased in such a way that Officer Law can supply what *he* knows about the incident.

Many times, there is an easy way to tell whether the prosecutor is leading his witness. If the question can be answered with a simple "yes" or "no," there is a good chance that it is leading. While this doesn't hold true in all cases, it's at least a good clue.

In addition, it's important to understand that lead- ing questions are prohibited, for the most part, only dur- ing direct examination. In contrast, they are usually al- lowed during cross-examination. They may also be allowed to establish unimportant or preliminary matters such as the name, residence or occupation of a witness during direct. Remember that each situation is different, and the judge ultimately makes the decision to either al- low or deny the use of leading questions.

2. Asked and Answered Questions. If, during direct examina- tion, the prosecutor asked his witness the same question over and over again, he may be doing so just to highlight the favorable points in his case. This type of "editorial emphasis" is usually viewed as being unfair. Therefore, if you see that it occurs, you should object to it. Keep in mind, however, that repetition is generally okay if it is done for the purpose of clarifying something a witness says. It is also permitted during cross-examination, at least to some extent, as a way to get an evasive witness to answer.

3. Questions That Assume Facts The Witness Did Not Testify To. This type of question is objectionable insofar as it asks a witness to *agree* to something that he didn't testify to. For example, imagine that the prosecutor asks his witness, Officer Law, the following question during direct exami- nation: "Officer, exactly how long had you been follow- ing the defendant when he swerved his car across the center line?" Notice here that the question *assumes* that Officer Law saw the defendant swerve his car—even though he might *not* have seen this! Thus, if Officer Law gives a simple answer such as "three blocks," he is, in effect, agreeing that the defendant swerved.

Keep in mind that this type of question is also objectionable during cross-examination. In view of this, you should always be on guard that the prosecutor doesn't ask them of you or your witnesses.

OBJECTIONS REGARDING THE ADMISSION OF AN EXHIBIT

The last chapter dealt with the principle that under normal circumstances, a foundation must first be established before an exhibit can be admitted into evidence. As you might imagine, this principle applies to the state just as much as it does to you. For example, in a speeding case that involves radar, the state normally attempts to introduce the speed measurements of the radar unit as an exhibit at trial. Now, before these measurements can be admitted into evidence, it is necessary that they are shown to be accurate. This is the foundation that must be established. (As you will see in Chapter 10, the state usually attempts to do this by showing that the radar unit was tested and the operator was qualified.) Thus, in most cases like this where the state has not adequately established the accuracy of the speed measurements, they simply cannot be used! In other words, they are not admitted into evidence.

Of course, there are many types of cases besides speeding where the state relies on exhibits to prove its case. For example, in driving under the influence cases, chemical test results are used. Or, in prosecutions for driving while suspended, the state often attempts to introduce affidavits of mailing or similar documents as exhibits.

Now, I hope you can see why it can be immensely beneficial to object to an exhibit if the proper foundation has not been established. Obviously, if your objection is successful, you can win this way. This is especially true if the exhibit is a critical part of the state's case, and this is not uncommon. On the other hand, if you don't object, you may be agreeing (or, in effect, stipulating) that the foundation is adequate and that the state's exhibit is okay to be admitted.

GENERAL SUGGESTIONS REGARDING OBJECTIONS

There is something that you should keep in mind if you decide to make an objection to an improper question. That is, it is best if you are quick and make your objection *before* the witness answers. If you can prevent the witness from answering, the judge will never get to hear the answer! This is good because the answer could be damaging to your case. However, if the witness has already answered, the judge might be psychologically influenced by the information, even though it may be inadmissible and must be stricken from the record.

Also keep in mind that the use of an objectionable question by the prosecutor, or the improper admission of an exhibit can sometimes be grounds for a reversal (or other remedy) if you appeal your case. However, understand that if you fail to make an objection to such improprieties at trial, you might be waiving (abandoning) your right to have them reviewed by a court of appeal. In other words, when you make an objection you are in effect preserving your right to have a higher court review your case. Moreover, if you find yourself in a situation where you are not sure whether to make an objection, you are generally better off to make it and protect your rights.

Here's one more thing to consider. Be aware that the prosecutor can object if *you* ask improper questions when you conduct a direct or cross-examination. That's why you should be careful not to ask any of the foregoing improper questions yourself. Remember, though, if you get into trouble, or you are unable to phrase a question properly, the judge should help you out.

HOW TO WIN BY USING TRIAL MOTIONS

Probably the simplest way of defining a trial motion is that it's a request that is addressed to the judge. In the sense that motions can usually be made verbally and informally at trial, they are similar to objections. Essentially, they can be made in order to accomplish a variety of objectives. As you might guess, there are so many different types of motions that conceivably could be made at a traffic hearing, our discussion must, for practical purposes, be narrowed down. Accordingly, I have taken a sampling of those that I feel you would most likely use at a traffic hearing and described them below.

MOTION TO DISMISS FOR LACK OF PROSECUTION

As you already know, the state has the obligation to initiate the prosecution of its case against you. In other words, if, for any reason, it is not in a position to prosecute you when your case is called, you can make a motion to dismiss your case for lack of prosecution. Then if you're lucky, you might have your case "thrown out." Of course, the state may not be in a position to prosecute for any number of reasons, but very commonly this situation arises when it has problems with its witnesses. For example, the investigating police officer may not show up in court to testify when he is supposed to.

As you might imagine, the judge may not dismiss your case on the first occasion that the state is not ready to prosecute. In fact, it's more likely that he will grant at least one continuance in order to give the state another chance to get its case ready. Obviously, the state has an interest in prosecuting traffic offenses (to promote high-way safety), and the judge must consider this before he dismisses a case. On the other hand, you, as a defendant, have a right to have your case heard promptly and without undue inconvenience. Essentially, then, it often boils down to a sort of "balancing test," where the judge bases his decision to grant a continuance on the overall fairness of the situation. Of course, if your case involves a minor speeding ticket, you should have a much better chance of having it dismissed initially than a more serious charge such as driving under the influence. (Note: I've had cases dismissed for lack of prosecution the first time around, but much more often, this has been the exception rather than the rule.)

Let me tell you something else that might help you. If your motion to dismiss is denied and the judge grants the state a continuance, you can ask him if he will designate the next court date as being a "firm" date. If you succeed, what that does is essentially *guarantee* that you will get your case dismissed if the state is unprepared the next time around.

MOTION TO DISMISS FOR LACK OF JURISDICTION—GEOGRAPHICAL

Before a traffic court can hear an offense, it ordinarily must occur within the *territory* served by that court. Otherwise, the court may not have the jurisdiction (legal authority) to prosecute. Essentially, this means that a "local" police officer (one who, unlike the state police, serves a particular locality), generally has no authority to write you a ticket if your offense occurs *outside* of the geographical boundaries of his locality. So, in such a situation, you could make a motion to dismiss your case for lack of geographical jurisdiction.

You should understand, however, that this motion will probably not be successful in a situation where a police officer sees you commit an offense in his locality, and then follows you in "hot pursuit" into another jurisdiction. When that is the case, a police officer is generally permitted to stop and ticket you outside the boundaries of his locality. In other words, the key is where your offense *occurs*, not necessarily where you are stopped.

MOTION TO DISMISS FOR LACK OF JURISDICTION—STATUTE OF LIMITATIONS

Statutes of limitations are laws that limit the amount of time the state has in which to enforce actions for traffic violations. Thus, if a traffic ticket is not *issued* against you within the statutory period of time after your offense, the court may not be able to prosecute you. For example, suppose that you are alleged to have been speeding on June 1, but you were not issued a ticket for that offense until July 10. Also assume that the statute of limitations in your state specifies that a speeding ticket cannot be issued more than thirty days after the date of the offense. Now in this situation, it is obvious that the statute of limitations has not been complied with because the ticket was issued more than thirty days after the offense. Accordingly, a motion to dismiss should be made.

It is necessary to find out what the statutory time period is that applies to your particular offense. Only then will you know for sure whether you have a chance to have your case dismissed. I say this because, in general, you can't depend on anyone else to recognize that you have a defense. Of course, there is a pretty good chance that the judge may see that you have a valid defense and dismiss your case. However, it is far safer to assume that the only one you can depend on to discover whether you have a defense is yourself.

MOTION TO DISMISS FOR THE STATE'S FAILURE TO PROVE A PRIMA FACIE CASE

In the normal course of events, a case is decided at trial only after both the state and the defense have had the opportunity to present their respective sides of the matter. As you have already learned, the state first puts on its witnesses, after which the defense does the same. Sometimes, however, this process is cut short, and the decision is made even before the defense begins its presentation. Why? Because *the state must make out a "prima facie" case. That is, one that on its face, could support a finding of guilt. If it fails to do this, the defense wins.* Thus, in such a situation, it's not even necessary for the defense to put on any witnesses, or for that matter, to proceed any further with its case.

Now in order to understand this concept fully, let's focus on what the state has to do in order to make out a *prima facie* case. Simply put, the state must introduce *some* evidence regarding each element (part) of the offense in question. For example, the offense of driving under the influence is basically comprised of the following elements: (1) the accused operated a motor vehicle, and (2) it was done while he was under the influence of intoxicating alcohol or drugs. In other words, the state will be unable to make out a *prima facie* case if it doesn't introduce at least *some* amount of evidence concerning each of these two essential elements.

Consider another example: imagine that you have been charged with speeding. At your hearing, assume that the state fails to introduce any evidence regarding the speed that your vehicle was traveling. Now in this situation, a *prima facie* case would obviously not be established. The reason for this is simple. Since the speed of your vehicle is an essential part of the offense, the state has the obligation to introduce some evidence in that regard.

Again, keep in mind that as long as the state introduces even a *minimal* amount of evidence concerning each of the essential elements of an offense, it will likely make out a *prima facie* case. In other words, it is only necessary for the state to show initially that a case *exists*. Once it does this, the case proceeds as usual through a full trial. Then at the end of the trial, the judge makes the ultimate determination as to whether the state has met its burden of proof (for example, proof beyond a reasonable doubt). Moreover, it's not uncommon for the state initially to make out a *prima facie* case, yet ultimately lose.

Let me also repeat here that it is essential to look up the statute or ordinance you are charged under. By reading the definition of the offense, you can determine what its elements are. In other words, you will then find out exactly what the state will be required to show in order to make out its *prima facie* case.

MOTION TO EXCLUDE WITNESSES FROM THE COURTROOM

As you might imagine, it can be a big plus to the state's case if its witnesses have the opportunity to listen to one another. For example, a witness can refresh his recollection and incorporate details that may have been forgotten if given the chance to first hear another witness' testimony. In fact, the witness can actually "adopt" another witness' version of the incident altogether. However, if a witness is not allowed to hear the testimony of the others, his or her testimony will be based primarily on what the witness knows about the case, not what some *other* witness knows about it.

With this in mind, you should now see what this motion is all about. Its main purpose is to prevent the state's witnesses from listening to each other's testimony in court by requiring them each to testify separately. This ensures that the testimony of each is not "colored" by what might be heard from other witnesses.

Moreover, if you are faced with a situation where the state intends to have more than one witness testify against you, make sure you consider the possible benefits of making this motion. Just keep in mind that if the judge grants your motion, he may also give the state the same opportunity to exclude your witnesses from the courtroom.

GENERAL SUGGESTIONS REGARDING MOTIONS

If you make a motion and the judge denies it, you may be able to make it again (renew it) later on in the hearing. It is always possible that the judge has denied your motion because he didn't have enough information to make a ruling at the time it was made. If additional information that supports your motion becomes available at some point later in your hearing, you may be able to get the judge to reconsider.

If you forget to make a motion at the appropriate time, it doesn't necessarily mean that you can't make it later on. For example, consider a case where the state has four individuals it plans to put on as witnesses. Assume that this would be a situation where it is desirable for you to make a motion to exclude those witnesses from the courtroom, but that you didn't realize this until after the first witness had finished testifying. Now, even though it would have been better to make the motion before any of the witnesses had testified, it still might be worthwhile to attempt it. In other words, always keep in mind the old cliche, "it's usually better late than never."

In addition, remember that by making a motion, you are preserving your right to have a higher court review your case should you ever desire to appeal. In other words, if the judge made an error in denying any motions you made at your trial, there is a possibility that a court of appeal would view this as a reason to give you a remedy, such as a reversal of the verdict or a retrial.

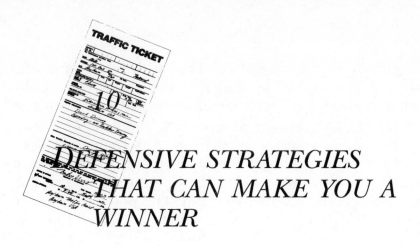

10
DEFENSIVE STRATEGIES THAT CAN MAKE YOU A WINNER

I suggested earlier that even though many motorists may have a perfectly legal defense to the traffic offense they are charged with, they might (and often do) fail to recognize this. As a result, they could be needlessly suffering many unpleasant consequences. In order to prevent this from happening to you, I have described in this chapter many of the specific defenses that can be used in a wide variety of common traffic violations.

Since there is a high degree of similarity regarding the way that traffic offenses are treated across the nation, most of the defenses that follow potentially can be used in any state. Of course the applicability of any given defense to your particular case will depend on the facts as well as the prevailing law.

Keep in mind that if you should find a defensive approach that you think might apply in your own case, it may be helpful or necessary to do some research into the law. This will allow you to see for sure if the defense you have chosen actually applies to your situation. In addition, knowing the law will give you the essential tools you need to argue your defense in court. Let me illustrate this by giving you a hypothetical example. Suppose that you have been charged with the offense of driving under the influence. Assume that at the time you were initially confronted by the police officer, you were merely sitting in a parked car on the side of the road with the engine off. Now, in a situation like this, it is likely that you would want to defend your case by showing that you were not "operating" the vehicle. Accordingly, you would be wise to check the case law in order to see how the courts have ruled on this issue: maybe it's *not* illegal to be sitting in a parked car with the engine off while intoxicated in the state where your offense occurred! The point is that you probably wouldn't know this unless you checked the law.

DRIVING UNDER THE INFLUENCE

OPERATION OF THE VEHICLE

If you were to read all of the DUI statutes across the country, you would find that most prohibit "operating" or "physically controlling" a vehicle as well as driving. In other words, it's not always necessary that one is found to be *actually* driving to be in violation of a DUI statute. In fact, the courts in some states hold that so long as a motorist demonstrates an intent to move a vehicle, he can be convicted of a DUI. (Note: For purposes of simplicity, the terms "operate" or "operation" will be used here interchangeably with the term "physically control" or any similar statutory terms that are used in the DUI statutes.)

Keep in mind that the courts from one state to another may differ somewhat in how they interpret the concept of what is meant by operating a vehicle. Some states give the concept a broad meaning, while others interpret it more narrowly. For example, in the case of State v. O'Toole, 673 S.W.2d 25 (Missouri), the defendant was discovered by the police asleep behind the wheel of his car with the engine running and the lights on. Even though the car was in "park" gear, the court decided that he was "operating" his vehicle, and found him guilty of driving while intoxicated.

On the other hand, an example of a more liberal view on this issue can be seen in the case of State vs. O'Malley, 416 A.2d 1387 (New Hampshire). There the defendant was found in an intoxicated condition asleep behind the wheel of a car that had its engine running and its lights on. He was then charged with a DUI and also with driving on the revoked list. At his hearing, the defendant testified that he started the car just to warm it up for someone else to drive him home, and then fell asleep at the wheel. The Supreme Court was of the opinion that he had no intent to move the vehicle and decided that he was not guilty.

To sum up, the important thing for you to understand is that the state must prove operation in order to convict you of a DUI offense. Thus, if you are charged with this offense, and there is some question as to whether you were "operating" a vehicle (in the legal sense), you may very well have a valid defense. Of course, your chances of success will depend largely on whether the governing law supports your position.

LOCATION OF THE OFFENSE

In some states, a DUI offense can be committed anywhere in the state, even in private locations. However, in others, the offense is limited mainly to the operation of a vehicle in *public areas*. For example, in the case of Rouse v. State, 651 S.W.2d 736 (Texas), the defendant was stopped and arrested for driving while intoxicated in a McDonald's parking lot. Since the law in Texas required that a vehicle be operated on a *public road*, he won his appeal and had his conviction reversed.

As you can see, depending on the law in the state where your defense occurs, it may be possible to defend yourself in a prosecution for a DUI by making the argument that you were not operating a vehicle in a location prohibited by the law. You can usually tell whether the statute under which you are charged will permit this argument by checking it's wording. As a general rule of thumb, if the statute specifies or implies that the offense can be committed *anywhere* in the state, it is then probable that private property is also included. But if the statute limits the offense to public highways or public areas, it may not be illegal to operate a vehicle, even while intoxicated, in certain private areas, such as parking lots, fields, or private roads.

TIME OF INTOXICATION

The gist of a DUI offense is that a person was intoxicated *while* driving a vehicle. This is why it's necessary for the state to prove that a person accused of this offense was intoxicated at the time he was operating a vehicle, and not at some other time. When the state is unable to establish this point at trial, it's usually grounds for a dismissal of the charge.

To illustrate this concept, consider a hypothetical example. Suppose that while driving your car in a completely sober condition, you were involved in an accident. Assume that afterwards, you walked into a nearby tavern and got drunk. Now assume that when you walked back to your car, a police officer (who was under the mistaken assumption that you had been under the influence at the time you were driving) charged you with a DUI. In such a situation, you might be able successfully to defend your case if you could convince the court that your drinking didn't occur until after your accident.

INTRODUCTION OF CHEMICAL BREATH TEST RESULTS

As you probably know, chemical breath testing is a method that is widely used throughout the nation in order to measure the blood alcohol content (BAC) of motorists charged with DUI offenses (although blood, urine, or saliva testing are sometimes employed as well). You may not know, however, that breath testing must be done in accordance with certain laws or regulations in order for the results to be valid. This is necessary to protect motorists from inaccurate test readings. Generally speaking, such laws or regulations require that: (1) breath-testing devices must be calibrated, inspected, and maintained, (2) operators who conduct breath tests must be properly trained and qualified, and (3) breath tests must be performed according to certain procedures. (Note: As a sample illustration of breath testing regulations, selected sections from the New Jersey Administrative Code have been reproduced in Appendix C.)

The important point to keep in mind is that in order to convict a motorist, the state must usually demonstrate that the legal requirements have been complied with, at least to a substantial degree. If it is unable to do this, a couple of things could happen: (1) the breath test results could be rendered completely invalid and incapable of being used as evidence, and (2) the test results could be given less weight as evidence. As you can see, it is possible to defend a DUI charge if you find out that the state has failed to comply with the applicable regulations.

The question you are now probably asking yourself is: "How can you show that the state has failed to comply with legal regulations?" Well, first of all, it is necessary to check the applicable statutes in order to familiarize yourself with the regulations in your jurisdiction. Only then will you know exactly what to look for. Secondly, when you are at trial, make sure that you closely inspect any documents that the state submits to show the validity of (lay a foundation for) the breath test readings. For example, if you examine the operator's training certificate, you can find out if the operator is properly certified. Likewise, by examining the inspection and maintenance reports for the testing device, you can see whether it was inspected and maintained in accordance with the law.

Remember that the state will be attempting to get such documents admitted into evidence as a foundation to prove that the test results are valid. However, if any of the documents do not show compliance with the law or if they are missing, there is a chance that the judge will not admit the breath test results into evidence. (Don't forget that any deficiencies in the state's proof might go undiscovered unless you point them out!) If you are unsure as to whether any particular document is in compliance with the law, you are probably better off objecting to its admission into evidence to be on the safe side and letting the judge decide whether it's okay or not. In other words, if you agree (stipulate) to the admission of a document, it gets admitted into evidence even though it may not be in compliance with the law.

I should also point out that the breath test results will probably be viewed as the single most important factor in determining whether you were intoxicated. Therefore, if the judge decides that they are invalid, there is a very good chance that the state will not be able to convict you.

RIGHT TO AN INDEPENDENT CHEMICAL TEST

The majority of states across the nation have statutes that say that a motorist charged with a DUI can have an independent BAC test performed *in addition* to the BAC tests performed by the police. (An example of such a statute is reproduced in Figure 10.1.) These statutes can give rise to a potential defense in the sense that if a motorist is denied access to an independent test, the state may not be able to use the results of the tests performed by the police at trial.

Keep in mind that under these statutes, it's not always essential that a motorist is given the *exact* assistance he asks for. Actually, the police generally fulfill their obligation so long as they give a motorist a reasonable oppor-

39-669.09. Drunken driving; choice of test; persons qualified to administer tests; privileges of person tested; results of test; available upon request. The law enforcement officer who requires a chemical blood, breath, or urine test pursuant to section 39-669.08 may direct whether the test shall be of blood, breath, or urine; *Provided*, that when the officer directs that the test shall be of a person's blood or urine, such person may choose whether the test shall be of his blood or urine. The person tested shall be permitted to have a physician of his choice evaluate his condition and perform or have performed whatever laboratory tests he deems appropriate in addition to and following the test administered at the direction of the law enforcement officer. If the officer shall refuse to permit such additional test to be taken, then the original test shall not be competent as evidence. Upon the request of the person tested, the results of the test taken at the direction of the law enforcement officer shall be made available to him.

FIGURE 10.1   NEBRASKA REVISED STATUTES

tunity to have an independent test performed. For instance, in the case of Ward V. State, 733 P.2d 625 (Alaska), the defendant told the police that he wanted an independent test to be performed at a particular hospital. The court decided, however, that the police officers were not required to take him to the hospital he preferred, since he was offered the choice of two other hospitals.

On the other hand, if the court decides that the police have not acted reasonably in complying with a motorist's request for an independent test, the police BAC tests are usually suppressed. For instance, in the case of State v. Hughes, 352 S.E.2d 643 (Georgia), the defendant asked the police to go to the Northside Hospital to have his independent test performed. Instead, the police transported him to Shallowford Hospital for the test. In view of the fact that the distance between the two hospitals was less than five miles, as well as the fact that the applicable statute gave a motorist the right to have an independent test administered by a qualified person of his own *choosing*, it was held that the police did not act reasonably under the circumstances. In other words, the police should have taken the defendant to the hospital *he* wanted to go to, and by not doing so, the defendant was able to suppress the use of the police BAC tests at his trial and win his case.

To sum up, you should be aware that you may have a possible defense if you are improperly denied your right to have an independent BAC test performed. If the judge decides that the police did not act reasonably, he may not allow the state to introduce the police BAC tests into evidence against you.

DELAY IN THE ADMINISTRATION OF THE CHEMICAL TESTS

Certain states have laws that specify that any chemical BAC tests must be performed within a specified amount of time after the offense in order to be valid. For instance, the Ohio Statute (See Figure 10.2) specifies that the court can admit evidence relating to chemical BAC tests *only if* a motorist is tested within two hours of the time of the violation.

The point to understand here is that if there has been any delay in the administration of your BAC tests, you should check to see if there is a statute similar to the above that might apply. In short, if you can show that the delay was more than that which is allowed by law, you may have a valid defense.

MEDICAL CONDITIONS

When a motorist is arrested for a DUI, it's common for the police to conduct a routine set of sobriety tests that measure such things as the person's balance, walking ability, speech, etc. (Note: Listed in Figure 10.3 is a standard form that is used by many police departments across the country to record information regarding the testing, ob-

§ 4511.19 Prohibition against driving while under the influence of alcohol or drugs or with certain concentration of alcohol in bodily substances; chemical analysis.

(A) No person shall operate any vehicle, streetcar, or trackless trolley within this state, if any of the following apply:

(1) The person is under the influence of alcohol, a drug of abuse, or alcohol and a drug of abuse;

(2) The person has a concentration of ten-hundredths of one per cent or more by weight of alcohol in his blood;

(3) The person has a concentration of ten-hundredths of one gram or more by weight of alcohol per two hundred ten liters of his breath;

(4) The person has a concentration of fourteen-hundredths of one gram or more by weight of alcohol per one hundred milliliters of his urine.

(B) In any criminal prosecution for a violation of this section, of a municipal ordinance relating to operating a vehicle while under the influence of alcohol, a drug of abuse, or alcohol and a drug of abuse, or of a municipal ordinance relating to operating a vehicle with a prohibited concentration of alcohol in the blood, breath, or urine, the court may admit evidence on the concentration of alcohol, drugs of abuse, or alcohol and drugs of abuse in the defendant's blood, breath, urine, or other bodily substance at the time of the alleged violation as shown by chemical analysis of the defendant's blood, urine, breath, or other bodily substance withdrawn within two hours of the time of the alleged violation.

When a person submits to a blood test at the request of a police officer under section 4511.191 [4511.19.1] of the Revised Code, only a physician, a registered nurse, or a qualified technician or chemist shall withdraw blood for the purpose of deter-

FIGURE 10.2   PAGE'S OHIO REVISED CODE ANNOTATED   *cont'd*

mining the alcohol, drug, or alcohol and drug content of the blood, if in his opinion the physical welfare of the person would be endangered by the withdrawing of blood.

Such bodily substance shall be analyzed in accordance with methods approved by the director of health by an individual possessing a valid permit issued by the director of health pursuant to section 3701.143 [3701.14.3] of the Revised Code.

If there was at the time the bodily substance was withdrawn a concentration of less than ten-hundredths of one per cent by weight of alcohol in the defendant's blood, less than ten-hundredths of one gram by weight of alcohol per two hundred ten liters of his breath, or less than fourteen-hundredths of one gram by weight of alcohol per one hundred milliliters of his urine, such fact may be considered with other competent evidence in determining the guilt or innocence of the defendant.

Upon the request of the person who was tested, the results of the chemical test shall be made available to him, his attorney, or his agent, immediately upon the completion of the chemical test analysis.

The person tested may have a physician, a registered nurse, or a qualified technician or chemist of his own choosing administer a chemical test or tests in addition to any administered at the request of a police officer, and shall be so advised. The failure or inability to obtain an additional chemical test by a person shall not preclude the admission of evidence relating to the chemical test or tests taken at the request of a police officer.

Any physician, registered nurse, or qualified technician or chemist who withdraws blood from a person pursuant to this section, and any hospital, first-aid station, or clinic at which blood is withdrawn from a person pursuant to this section, is immune from criminal liability, and from civil liability that is based upon a claim of assault and battery or based upon any other claim that is not in the nature of a claim of malpractice, for any act performed in withdrawing blood from the person.

FIGURE 10.2   PAGE'S OHIO REVISED CODE ANNOTATED

servations, etc. of a driver who is suspected of drunk driving. It will give you a good idea of the various types of routine tests that are used.) The primary reason why such tests are given is to supply the state with evidence that the accused *appeared* to be intoxicated. The truth of the matter is, however, that a person does not have to be under the influence of an intoxicating substance in order to appear intoxicated. On the contrary, a person who looks that way might only be exhibiting the symptoms of a disease, a physical condition, or the effects of a medication. For example, someone who has cerebellar disease might do poorly while performing balance tests, since incoordination is a common symptom of this condition. (Note: For a comprehensive list of symptoms that are produced by alcohol as well as by other pathological conditions, see Appendix B.)

The main point to understand here is that if you are charged with a DUI, and the state is unable to prove that you were under the influence of an *intoxicating substance*, you might be able to get your case dismissed. In other words, you may have a defense if you can demonstrate that your intoxicated appearance (or uncoordinated actions) resulted from a medical condition, and *not* from an intoxicating substance, such as alcohol. (Note: In order to furnish satisfactory proof of your medical condition, it may be necessary to supply the court with a letter from your physician or possibly have him come to court in person to testify.)

I should mention that this approach may not be enough *in itself* to win your case, especially if the state has introduced successfully the results of chemical BAC tests against you. This is largely because such tests are generally viewed as strong proof of intoxication and are often difficult to counteract. Nevertheless, in a situation where the test readings are "borderline," or where they are not available, this approach can certainly tip the scales in your favor.

National Safety Council

ALCOHOL INFLUENCE REPORT FORM

Subject Name		Street Address		
City, State, Zip		Date of Birth	Sex ☐ Male ☐ Female	Weight
Driver License No.	State	Date Arrested	Time	Ticket No.

OBSERVATIONS

Odor Of Alcoholic Beverage
☐ None   ☐ Moderate   ☐ Strong   Describe:

Clothing Description/Condition
☐ Neat   ☐ Disorderly   ☐ Soiled   Describe:

Attitude
☐ Polite   ☐ Belligerent   Comments:
☐ Cooperative   ☐ Combative

Speech
☐ Good   ☐ Fair   ☐ Poor   Comments:

List Any Unusual Actions/Statements

Visible Signs Of Illness/Injury

PERFORMANCE TEST

Balance (one leg stand)
☐ Good   ☐ Fair   ☐ Swaying   ☐ Use Arms   ☐ Hopping   ☐ Puts Foot Down   ☐ **Fails Test**

Walking (walk and turn test)			Score ___		Finger to Nose Test
☐ Good	☐ Loses balance during instructions	☐ Starts early	☐ Pauses for balance	☐ Uses arms	☐ Right ☐ Left
☐ Not touching heel to toe	☐ Steps off line	☐ Incorrect number of steps	☐ Turns improperly	☐ **Fails Test**	

Horizontal Gaze (Nystagmus Test)   Score ___

☐ Right eye not following smoothly   ☐ Right eye jerking at maximum deviation   ☐ Right eye jerks before 45°   ☐ OK

☐ Left eye not following smoothly   ☐ Left eye jerking at maximum deviation   ☐ Left eye jerks before 45°   ☐ OK

☐ Pass   ☐ Fail

Instruction (comprehension)
☐ Good   ☐ Fair   ☐ Poor   Comment:

Remarks/Other Test Results

NYSTAGMUS

	0	1	2	3	4	5	6
0							
1							
2							
3							
4							
5							
6							
7							
8							
9							

► Time of Tests ___

OBSERVER'S OPINION

Under the Influence of Alcohol   ☐ Yes   ☐ No   Ability to Drive Impaired   ☐ Yes   ☐ No

Comments:

► See Reverse

FIGURE 10.3   *cont'd*

Subject Name

MIRANDA WARNING

The U.S. Supreme Court requires me to inform you that:

1. You have a right to remain silent.
2. Anything you say is evidence and may be used against you in court.
3. You are entitled to a lawyer and to have him present now or anytime during questioning.
4. If you cannot afford a lawyer, one will be appointed for you without cost.

Do you understand your rights ☐ No ☐ Yes
Are you willing to talk to me ☐ No ☐ Yes

INTERVIEW

To Be Completed ▶ By Interviewer	Time	Day	Date	Badge No.	City/County

Driving

Were you driving a motor vehicle ☐ No ☐ Yes	Destination	Direction	What Roadway	Point of Origin

Start Time	Current Time	Vehicle Type	Model	Other Related Statements From Driver

Drinking

Have You Been Drinking ☐ No ☐ Yes	Where		What

How Much		Time Started	Time Stopped

Accident

Have You Been In An Accident Today ☐ No ☐ Yes	Any Alcohol Since The Accident ☐ No ☐ Yes	If So, What

Where		Time Started	Time Stopped

Injuries/Disabilities

Do You Have Any Injuries or Physical Disabilities ☐ No ☐ Yes (Describe)	Do You Have Any Illnesses ☐ No ☐ Yes (Describe)

Medical

Any Recent Medical or Dental Care ☐ No ☐ Yes (Describe)	Are You Taking Any Medications (prescription/over the counter) ☐ No ☐ Yes (Describe)	
		If so, time of last dosage

Have You Been Using Marijuana ☐ No ☐ Yes	When	Any Other Controlled Substances ☐ No ☐ Yes (What)	When

Food/Sleep

When Did You Last Eat	What	Did The Alcohol You Consumed Affect Your Ability To Drive ☐ No ☐ Yes

When Did You Last Sleep	How Long

General Comments/Remarks

Time Interview Completed	Date	Signature of Officer

5M988　　　　Printed in U.S.A.　　　　321.98
©1988 National Safety Council

FIGURE 10.3

MISTAKEN IDENTITY OF THE DRIVER

This topic is discussed under this heading in the section on Moving Violations in General later in this chapter.

SPEEDING

MISTAKEN VEHICLE

Radar is a very popular tool used in the prosecution of speeding offenses. While it is generally considered to be reliable, it's not infallible. For example, one of the major limitations of a radar unit is that it is sometimes difficult for the person operating it to be sure that he is targeting (identifying) the *correct* vehicle. As a matter of fact, when the density of traffic increases, so do the chances that there will be an error in selection.

If you happen to be fighting a speeding ticket, this limitation in the operation of radar could serve as the basis for a valid defense. Here, the key would be to show that there might have been an error in the selection of your vehicle. Your job would be to cross-examine the radar operator to see if he might have mistakenly targeted your vehicle instead of the actual vehicle that was speeding. If you are able to create some doubt regarding the issue of whether yours is the vehicle that was targeted, it might be enough to defeat the state's case.

ACCURACY OF THE SPEED MEASUREMENTS

In a prosecution for speeding, the state has the obligation to show that any speed measurements obtained by radar are accurate. That is to say that it must lay a foundation before the measurements can be admitted into evidence against a motorist. In order to demonstrate accuracy, the state is, generally speaking, required to show the following: (1) that the radar unit was tested and/or calibrated, (2) that the testing procedure was acceptable, and (3) that the radar operator knew how to use the unit.

Now the key to this defensive approach is to show that the state has failed to satisfy one or more of the above requirements, and thereby prevent the speed measurements from being used as evidence against you. In order to do this, it is necessary to follow a procedure similar to that discussed in the section on Introduction of Breath Test Results. In other words, you should first check the applicable law so that you are familiar with the requirements for the admission of radar speed measurements. Then at trial, you should inspect any documents that the state submits for the purpose of laying a foundation for the admission of the speed measurements, such as certificates that indicate operator training or calibration of the radar unit. If any documents are missing, or if they show that the law has not been complied with, the judge may not allow the state to introduce the speed measurements into evidence. Once again, if you are unsure as to whether there has been compliance, it's good to play it safe. In other words, object and let the judge decide if there is a problem. Obviously, he knows the law better than you do and should know if there is some deficiency in the state's proof.

It should also be mentioned that the state might attempt to prove its case by submitting speed measurements obtained from a speedometer. If this is the situation, you should make sure that the speedometer used was properly calibrated and/or inspected. Obviously, if there is no proof of the speedometer's accuracy, you can argue that the speed measurements should not be admitted into evidence.

Finally, you should be aware that speed measurements are sometimes admitted into evidence even though their accuracy may be questionable. If that happens, it might help to make the argument that the measurements should not be given much weight as evidence. Needless to say, it is much better if the judge does not allow the state to use them at all, since that will almost guarantee that you will win your case.

ESTABLISHMENT OF THE SPEED ZONE

Some jurisdictions require that adequate signs must be posted that warn motorists of the speed limit when it is lower than the statewide maximum. When signs are not properly posted, the traffic courts generally hold that the lower speed limit is invalid and the higher statewide limit applies. To illustrate, consider a hypothetical example. Let's say that you are accused of going 50 mph in a 35 mph zone. Assume, however, that the road you were traveling on did not have any signs that specified that the speed limit was 35 mph. Now in a situation like this, the court could disregard the 35 mph limit and apply the statewide limit. Assuming then, that the statewide limit is 55 mph, your speed of 50 mph would not be in violation of the law.

In addition, it may also be a defense if the signs are not *adequately* posted. That is to say that the signs are not reasonably likely to give actual notice of the speed limit. For instance, in the case of People v. Churnton, 324 N.Y.S.2d 500 (New York), the defendant was charged with going 38 mph in a 25 mph zone. The defense, he argued, was that the 25 mph zone was invalid since he passed only one poorly visible 25 mph sign. In other words, besides being the wrong size, there also were not enough signs posted along the roadway. This argument was successful, and the court held that a municipality has a duty to inform correctly the traveling public of the speed limit before it can enforce its speed laws.

In sum, if the facts of your case suggest that you might be able to use either of the above approaches, check the law to see if the jurisdiction where your offense occurred requires the adequate posting of signs. Assuming that it does, you might be able to defend your case by arguing at trial that you did not have proper notice of the speed limit. If the state cannot show that signs were adequately posted in accordance with the law, you will stand a good chance to win your case.

INTENT

Driving at excessive speed does not always amount to a violation of the law, unless it is done with intent (voluntarily). In other words, if your speeding resulted from an occurrence over which you had *no control*, you may be able to defend your case by arguing that you had no intent to speed. An example of this concept can be seen in the case of State v. Weller, 230 A.2d 242 (Connecticut). In that situation, the court decided that the defendant had no intent to speed because a spring that closed the throttle plate in his car broke and caused it to go 80 mph.

The distinction should be made here that if you are in a situation where it is possible to somehow avoid speeding, this defense does not usually apply. For instance, in State v. Baker, 571 P.2d 65 (Kansas), the court held that the malfunction of the defendant's cruise control device was not a valid defense since it was something that he had control over. That is to say, he could have simply applied his brakes and avoided speeding.

LEGAL JUSTIFICATION

Speeding, as well as various other traffic offenses, can be excused or legally justified under certain circumstances. To illustrate, let's take a look at the four basic defenses that make up the category of legal justification.

1. Self defense and defense of others. This defense might apply if you can show that your speeding was reasonably done in response to a real or perceived threat to your own safety or the safety of others. For example, in the case of Cooper v. District of Columbia, 183 A.2d 557 (Washington, D.C.), the defendant, who was with his wife and two young children, was being followed by a vehicle on a dark, rainy night. He didn't know that the vehicle following him was a police car, but instead thought that it was occupied by ill-intentioned persons, due to the fact that it was following him very closely and blinding him with its headlights. This led him to exceed the speed limit in an attempt to escape from the pursuing vehicle. On his appeal for a speeding conviction, the defendant was able to win his case by arguing that he was put in fear for his and his family's safety. In short, the court concluded that his fear was justified under the circumstances.

2. Necessity. This defense could come into play if you must exceed the speed limit in order to avoid an emergency. For example, in a New York case, the defendant sped up to 67 mph in a 50 mph zone in order to pass around and avoid colliding with a car that was rapidly slowing down in front of him. The court held that he had not violated the speeding statute because under the circumstances, speeding was a necessity. In other words, it was the *only way* he could have avoided the emergency situation that faced him. People v. Catalvo, 316 N.Y.S.2d 873 (New York).

Keep in mind, however, that this defense is normally rejected if: (1) you were responsible for creating the emergency situation, or (2) there was an alternative to speeding that you could have taken but didn't.

3. Entrapment. If you are involved in a situation where a police officer *induces* you to commit a speeding offense, you might be able to win by arguing that you were entrapped. For example, in the case of State v. Brown, 318 N.W.2d 370 (Wisconsin), the defendant saw a vehicle approaching the rear of his car that was driving erratically and approaching at a high rate of speed. In order to get away from the approaching vehicle (which he didn't know was driven by a police officer), and to avoid a possible physical confrontation, he accelerated to 72 mph. Here, the court excused the defendant's speeding since it was caused by the actions of the police officer.

4. Coercion/Duress. Coercion or duress is very similar to the preceeding three categories that fall under the heading of legal justification. In essence, this defense could apply in any situation that involves the following elements: a) you are threatened with serious bodily injury or death, b) you have a legitimate belief that the threat will be carried out, and c) there is no reasonable way to escape the threatened harm except by violating a traffic law.

BREAKING THE SPEED LIMIT "LEGALLY"

I know this sounds hard to believe, but in about a quarter of the states, driving in excess of the posted speed limit is not always illegal! In other words if your speeding occurs in a jurisdiction that has a *prima facie* speed statute, the law only creates a *legal presumption* that exceeding the posted limit is excessive. Thus it may be possible to overcome this presumption at trial if you can introduce evidence to show that your speed, even though it was over the limit, was warranted under the circumstances.

For example, in the case of State v. Nedelkoff, 263 N.E.2d 803 (Ohio), the defendant was found to be traveling 60 mph in a 45 mph zone, yet he was not convicted of speeding. Simply put, the court decided that 60 mph was *reasonable under the circumstances*. The primary factors on which it based its decision were that the defendant had a straight road, the traffic was light, and the weather was good. In other words, even though there was a presumption that any speed over 45 mph was excessive, this presumption was overcome (rebutted) by the defendant.

Keep in mind that about three quarters of the states have adopted statutes that have "fixed" maximum speed limits rather than *prima facie* statutes. Now these laws differ in the sense that under a "fixed" speed law, it is *conclusively* unlawful to exceed the speed limit. Hence, it is not possible to argue that exceeding the speed limit was reasonable under the circumstances in these jurisdictions.

Obviously, this defensive approach depends on whether the statute you are charged under is *prima facie* or fixed. Therefore, in order to help you to recognize the difference between these two types of laws, the speeding statutes from Arizona and Delaware have been reproduced in Figures 10.4 and 10.5 respectively. Notice that the underlined portions of the Arizona statute, which is a *prima facie* statute, refers to speed in excess of the limit as being *prima facie evidence* of unlawful speed, while the Delaware statute, which has fixed speed limits, leaves no doubt that speed in excess of the limit is illegal.

MISTAKEN IDENTITY OF THE DRIVER

You can defend a speeding offense by showing that you were not the driver of the vehicle that was speeding. For a discussion of this topic, please refer to this heading in the section on Moving Violations in General, later in this chapter.

DRIVING WHILE SUSPENDED

NOTICE OF THE SUSPENSION

In prosecutions for the offense of driving while suspended (DWS), an important issue that frequently comes up at trial is whether the Department of Motor Vehicles (DMV) properly notified the defendant that his driving privileges were suspended. Indeed, in most cases, if the state is not able to prove that proper notice was given, it

§ 28–701.   **Reasonable and prudent speed; prima facie evidence; exceptions**

A.   A person shall not drive a vehicle on a highway at a speed greater than is reasonable and prudent under the circumstances, conditions and actual and potential hazards then existing.   In every event, speed shall be so controlled as may be necessary to avoid colliding with any object, person, vehicle or other conveyance on, entering or adjacent to the highway in compliance with legal requirements and the duty of all persons to exercise reasonable care for the protection of others.

B.   Except as provided in subsections C and D or where a special hazard requires a lesser speed, any speed in excess of these speeds is prima facie evidence that the speed is too great and therefore unreasonable:

1.   Fifteen miles per hour approaching school crossing.

2.   Twenty-five miles per hour in any business or residential district.

3.   Sixty-five miles per hour in other locations.

C.   The speed limits set forth in this section may be altered as authorized in §§ 28–702 and 28–703.

D.   The maximum speed as provided in this section shall be reduced to that which is reasonable and prudent under the conditions and having regard to the actual and potential hazards then existing, such as when:

1.   Approaching and crossing an intersection or railroad crossing.

2.   Approaching and going around a curve.

3.   Approaching a hill crest.

4.   Traveling upon any narrow or winding roadway.

5.   Special hazards exist with respect to pedestrians or other traffic or by reason of weather or highway conditions.

E.   A person shall not drive a motor vehicle at a speed that is less than that which is reasonable and prudent under existing conditions.

FIGURE 10.4   ARIZONA REVISED STATUTES ANNOTATED

is usually unable to obtain a conviction. For example, in the case of People v. Walsh, 367 N.Y.S.2d 168 (New York), the defendant had his DWS charge dismissed because the state failed to produce evidence showing that the notice of suspension was ever mailed to him. Even though the state actually produced the letter of revocation, it didn't produce any document, such as an affidavit of mailing to show that the notice letter was actually sent in the mail.

§ 4169. Specific speed limits; penalty.

(a) Where no special hazard exists, the following speeds shall be lawful, but any speed in excess of such limits shall be absolute evidence that the speed is not reasonable or prudent and that it is unlawful:

    (1) All types of vehicles:

        a. 25 miles per hour in any business district;

        b. 25 miles per hour in any residential district;

        c. 20 miles per hour at all school crossings where 20 mph regulatory signs are in effect during specific periods;

        d. 50 miles per hour on 2-lane roadways;

        e. 55 miles per hour on 4-lane roadways and on divided roadways.

(b) Whenever the Department of Transportation shall determine, on the basis of engineering studies and traffic investigations or upon the basis of a federal law or directive by the Congress or the President, that a maximum speed limit set pursuant to subsection (a) of this section in any particular place on the state maintained highway system is greater or less than is reasonable or safe, the Department shall declare a reasonable and safe maximum limit thereat, which limit shall be effective when posted. Such maximum limit may be declared to be effective either part or all of the time and differing limits may be established for different times of the day, for different types of vehicles, for different weather conditions and when other significant factors differ. Such maximum limits may be posted on fixed or variable signs. Any speed in excess of such displayed limits shall be absolute evidence that the speed is not reasonable or prudent and that it is unlawful.

(c) Penalties for violation of this section are as follows:

    (1) Whoever violates this section shall for the first offense be fined $20. For each subsequent offense, he shall be fined $25 or be imprisoned not less than 10 nor more than 30 days, or both. A subsequent violation, before being punishable as such, shall have been committed within 24 months after the commission of the prior offense.

    (2) Any person violating this section who exceeds the maximum speed limit by more than 5 miles per hour but less than 16 miles per hour shall pay an additional fine of $1 per mile, if such violation is a first offense, or $2 per mile, if such violation is a subsequent offense, for each mile in excess of the maximum speed limit.

    (3) Any person violating this section who exceeds the maximum speed limit by more than 15 miles per hour but less than 20 miles per hour shall pay an additional fine of $2 per mile, if such violation is a first offense, or $3 per mile, if such violation is a subsequent offense, for each mile in excess of the maximum speed limit.

    (4) Any person violating this section who exceeds the maximum speed limit by more than 19 miles per hour shall pay an additional fine of $3 per mile, if such violation is a first offense, or $4 per mile, if such violation is a second offense, for each mile in excess of the maximum speed limit.

FIGURE 10.5 DELAWARE CODE ANNOTATED

Now in order to be successful in using this approach, you have to show that you were not properly notified of your suspension by the DMV. Your strategy, therefore, would be to examine the state's evidence at trial to see if there are any deficiencies in its proof. For example, was notice ever mailed to you? Was it mailed to your correct address? Or, was it mailed to some other individual with a similar name? In sum, if it appears that the DMV failed to provide you with adequate notice, it is unlikely that the state will be able to convict you.

It should be pointed out also that in most states the DMV can give notice simply by sending it by regular or certified mail to a person's last known address. So, if this is the law in your jurisdiction, it wouldn't matter if you didn't actually *receive* notice. The state would most likely be able to prove its case just by showing that notice was mailed. However, some states require that the DMV has to obtain a signed return receipt, or else take additional steps to ensure that notice is received.

In sum, it's important to check the statute that spells out the kind of notice required. Then you will be able to know for sure whether the DMV gave you sufficient notice as required by law.

LEGALITY OF THE SUSPENSION

Motorists are sometimes mistakenly classified as having other driving privileges suspended, when in fact, they should not be listed in that category at all. This can occur for a variety of reasons. For example, a motorist might be placed on the suspended list because of a computer error. Or, what sometimes happens is that the DMV fails to remove a motorist from the suspended status when it should. The point is, however, that even though motorists may be on the suspended list by mistake, they can still be charged with a DWS if they are stopped by a police officer.

Now, if this should happen to you, you can defend your case if you can show the judge that your suspension was improper. Essentially, this involves contacting the DMV in order to obtain a letter (or some form of *written* proof) that indicates that you were improperly listed as a suspended driver on the date you were stopped for the DWS offense. In short, if the judge is satisfied that your suspension was invalid, you should win your case.

Be aware that it may be difficult to get the written documentation from the DMV in time for your trial date. (I don't have to tell you that dealing with a large bureaucracy like the DMV is usually enough to drive a person half crazy.) So if that is the case, I suggest that you call or write the court clerk and ask for a continuance. If you explain that you are waiting to get documentation from the DMV that is essential to the defense of your case, you shouldn't have any trouble getting some additional time.

OPERATION OF THE VEHICLE

A DWS can be defended by showing that you were not "operating" a vehicle. For a discussion of the topic, see this heading in the section on DUI, earlier in this chapter.

LOCATION OF THE OFFENSE

In some jurisdictions, a DWS can be defended by showing that the driving was not done on a public road or area. For a discussion of this topic, see this heading in the earlier section on DUI.

NECESSITY

This defense can sometimes be used in a prosecution for DWS under appropriate circumstances. For a discussion of the concept of necessity, see the heading entitled Legal Justification in the section on speeding, earlier in this chapter.

MISTAKEN IDENTITY OF THE DRIVER

For a discussion of this topic, see this heading in the next section, Moving Violations in General.

MOVING VIOLATIONS IN GENERAL

All moving traffic violations are similar in the sense that they are essentially based upon the visual observation of a witness. Due to this similarity, certain defensive approaches can apply almost universally under appropriate circumstances. The defensive approaches described in this section can apply to virtually any moving violation which falls into the following general categories:

1. Careless or reckless driving
2. Tailgating or following too closely
3. Delaying or obstructing traffic
4. Improper passing
5. Improper turning
6. Improper backing
7. Failure to stop
8. Failure to give signals
9. Failure to observe traffic signs or signals
10. Failure to observe directions of a police officer
11. Failure to yield to pedestrians or other vehicles
12. Failure to observe the right of way

MISTAKEN CONCLUSION

You can defend yourself in a prosecution for a moving violation if you can show that the witnesses who testify for the state are mistaken in their conclusions. (This is nothing you don't already know, but I think it is worthy of repeating.) The point is that you only need to create some doubt in the judge's mind in order to succeed. In other words, the judge does not have to be totally convinced that your version of the facts is correct. Just as long as you can create some doubt about the conclusions of the state's witnesses, it is possible to have your case dismissed.

INTENT

For a discussion on this topic, see this heading in the earlier section on Speeding.

LEGAL JUSTIFICATION

For a discussion of this topic, see this heading in the earlier section on Speeding.

MISTAKEN IDENTITY OF THE DRIVER

When the state prosecutes a case for a moving violation, it must show that the person accused of the offense, not someone else, was the driver of the vehicle at the time of the violation. Generally speaking, the method by which it does this is by having a witness (usually the investigating police officer) make a visual courtroom identification of the defendant, confirming him as the driver. There is a good chance, however, for the defendant to win where it appears that the state's identification could be a mistake.

By the same token, a defensive approach you can take at trial is to show that the witness who has identified you is mistaken. One way of doing this is by attacking the credibility of that witness through cross-examination. To illustrate, consider the following hypothetical situation. Let's say that someone who had access to your car committed a moving violation and exhibited your driving credentials to Officer Law. Assume that you were then given a ticket for a violation you did not commit. Also assume that between the time of the offense and the court hearing, you changed your appearance by growing a moustache and a beard. Now, if Officer Law identified you in court as the driver, you could cast some doubt on his identification by showing that he was not aware of any change in your appearance. Here is an example of how you might cross-examine him to establish this:

> *You:* Officer, do you remember what I looked like at the time the offense was committed?
>
> *Officer Law:* Yes, about the same as you do now.
>
> *You:* Are you sure?
>
> *Officer Law:* Yes.

Now here's the clincher: If after cross-examining Officer Law, you could then convince the judge that you did not have a beard and moustache on the date of the offense, the judge might think that Officer Law was confusing you for another individual.

Another way to cast doubt on an in-court identification is to establish an alibi. For example, if you could show that you were at work at the time the offense was committed, it certainly would make it appear doubtful that you were the driver.

Keep in mind, however, that if you were to use either of the approaches described above, it would probably be important to have witnesses who could support your testimony. Let me caution you that most judges might not be convinced by your testimony alone. In sum, the more doubt you can raise regarding the issue of your identity, the more you can influence a decision in your favor.

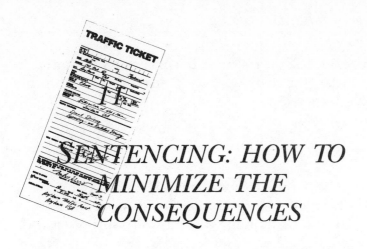

SENTENCING: HOW TO MINIMIZE THE CONSEQUENCES

This book is intended to give you the necessary tools to enable you to win your case and thus avoid sentencing altogether. However, the harsh reality is that winning is not always guaranteed—no matter how well your case is prepared or presented. Even skilled and experienced trial lawyers lose once in a while. Moreover, *even if you are not successful in getting your case dismissed completely, there may be other options available that can at least help to minimize some of the unpleasant consequences.*

Listed below are several kinds of special requests that you might be able to benefit from, subject, of course, to their availability in your particular traffic court.

INSTALLMENT PLANS

If you are given a fine, it may be possible to pay it off over an extended period, rather than in one lump sum. In order to get an installment plan, however, it will probably be necessary to convince the judge that a lump sum payment would create a financial hardship for you. Since the judge may ask you questions regarding your ability to pay the fine, I would suggest that you prepare a list showing your monthly income and expenses. Then you can easily determine how much you can afford to pay comfortably each month toward your fine.

Figure 11.1 is an outline that has been included in order to assist you in preparing a list of your monthly income and expenses.

REDUCED PENALTIES

Sometimes motor vehicle laws provide for a fixed penalty that cannot be modified by the judge. However, there are also laws that allow the judge discretion to impose a wide range of penalties. For instance, take a look at Figure

```
INCOME
    Total from all sources:                          $_____


EXPENSES
    Mortgage/rent
    Utilities
    Telephone
    Food (groceries, restaurants, etc.)
    Home maintenance
    Insurance (Health, Auto, Life, etc.)
    Medical/Dental
    Car payments
    Car repairs/maintenance
    Gasoline
    Clothing
    Recreation
    Vacations
    Miscellaneous
    Total                                            $_____



Balance (Income less Expenses):                      $_____




(Note:  Monthly installment payments for traffic fines
        should not exceed the balance amount indicated
        above).
```

FIGURE 11.1   WORKSHEET FOR COMPUTING MONTHLY INCOME/EXPENSES

11.2, which is a reproduction of the reckless driving statute in Connecticut. Notice that the potential penalties for a first offense range anywhere from a $100.00 fine all the way up to a $300.00 fine *and* thirty days in jail.

Now assuming that the judge has discretion in sentencing you, the point is that he may be more lenient if you remind him of any applicable "mitigating" (alleviating) circumstances. For example, suppose that you are being tried for reckless driving under a statute similar to the one illustrated in Figure 11.2. Let's also say that at the time of the incident, you were rushing to get to the emergency room because your passenger was sick. Now, even though these circumstances may not be a complete defense to the charge of reckless driving, they might induce the judge to give you a very light sentence.

---

§ 14–222. Reckless driving

(a) No person shall operate any motor vehicle upon any public highway of the state, or any road of any specially chartered municipal association or of any district organized under the provisions of chapter 105,[1] a purpose of which is the construction and maintenance of roads and sidewalks, or in any parking area for ten cars or more or upon any private road on which a speed limit has been established in accordance with the provisions of section 14–218a or upon any school property recklessly, having regard to the width, traffic and use of such highway, road, school property or parking area, the intersection of streets and the weather conditions. The operation of a motor vehicle upon any such highway, road or parking area for ten cars or more at such a rate of speed as to endanger the life of any person other than the operator of such motor vehicle, or the operation, downgrade, upon any highway, of any commercial motor vehicle with the clutch or gears disengaged, or the operation knowingly of a motor vehicle with defective mechanism, shall constitute a violation of the provisions of this section.

(b) Any person who violates any provision of this section shall be fined not less than one hundred dollars nor more than three hundred dollars or imprisoned not more than thirty days or be both fined and imprisoned for the first offense and for each subsequent offense shall be fined not more than six hundred dollars or imprisoned not more than one year or be both fined and imprisoned.

FIGURE 11.2 CONNECTICUT GENERAL STATUTES ANNOTATED

Consider another example. Suppose that you are being tried for speeding. Assume, however, that at the time of the incident, your speedometer was broken. If you remind the judge of this fact before you are sentenced, he might take it into consideration in giving you a light penalty. Don't forget, however, that your success would probably depend on the length of time that your speedometer was broken. In other words, if you neglected to fix it for a long period of time, the judge would probably not feel too sympathetic.

WORK RELEASE

If your sentence requires you to serve time in jail, the judge may allow you to serve your time on weekends, or at times that do not interfere with your opportunity to work and earn a living. Now if the judge in your traffic court is like most, he should be more inclined to permit this if he thinks that you might lose your job. Hence, if there is any possibility that your job security will be threatened by taking time off to serve jail time, you should let the judge know about it. Judges usually try to avoid creating a situation where an individual (or, especially a family) is forced into financial hardship.

LIMITED DRIVING PRIVILEGES

It may be possible to get permission to drive on a limited or restricted basis if you lose your driving privileges. For instance, a statute in Florida (Florida Statutes Annotated, Sec. 322.71 [2]) specifies that motorists who have lost their driving privileges may be eligible to drive on a restricted basis for employment or business purposes only. These restricted privileges are sometimes granted in cases where motorists show that their license suspension will cause a serious hardship and interfere with their livelihood.

Since similar laws exist in other states, you should always check to see if one might apply to your particular situation. If you are allowed to drive on a limited basis, many of the problems associated with a complete loss of driving privileges can be greatly minimized.

REHABILITATIVE ALTERNATIVES

Some motor vehicle statutes provide for rehabilitative alternatives as a substitute for imprisonment or other penalties in cases involving driving under the influence. For instance, motorists convicted of this offense in New Jersey can usually satisfy any jail term that is imposed by attending a rehabilitation program instead. In such cases, the court orders the motorist to attend a facility wherein he is given alcohol education and/or treatment.

The point to understand here is that if you are convicted of driving under the influence, you should check the law to see if any similar rehabilitation programs exist in your jurisdiction. Indeed, you may find that such a program is much more desirable than serving your sentence in jail.

Keep in mind, however, that it may be left to the judge's discretion as to whether a rehabilitation program is warranted in your case. In view of this, you might benefit by showing the judge that such an alternative would be in your "best interests." For example, if you could demonstrate that you have a legitimate alcohol problem, the judge would probably think that treatment would be more helpful to you than punishment. (Note: If you want to prove that you have an alcohol problem, I suggest that you either bring a physician into court or else have him write a letter to verify this. I think it is safe to say that a physician's word would be more convincing than your own in this regard.)

TAKING YOUR CASE TO A HIGHER COURT

Even though the subject of an appeal is beyond the scope of this book, I think it is important for you to know a few essentials about appeals. The first thing you will have to do is to decide whether an appeal is going to be worthwhile. In order to make this decision, you should know a little about the positive and negative aspects of an appeal. Let's start with the positive aspects. Consider that if you win an appeal, you will be given a remedy. For example, you might have your conviction reversed (set aside), or perhaps you may get a new trial. In addition to these potential remedies, you should be given the opportunity to have your sentence "put on hold" (suspended) pending the outcome of your appeal.

But there are negative aspects. You must consider that the odds of winning are usually against you. Generally speaking, the only way you can win an appeal is if: (1) the evidence introduced at trial was not sufficient to support the decision, or (2) the judge made an error such as refusing to grant a motion you may have made, which was prejudicial to your rights. (Mind you, not *all* errors are considered to be prejudicial. An error may be "harmless," in which case it does not constitute grounds for relief.)

I'll admit that the question of whether to appeal or not may not be an easy one to answer. Obviously, if you feel that the traffic court decision was unfair, you might want to do something about it. However, I'm sure you don't want to go through the trouble and expense of appealing if it's not going to do you any good. That's why I recommend that you speak with an attorney if you are considering an appeal. At least that way you can get a professional's opinion of what your chances are of winning. Also, if you decide to go ahead with an appeal, you will probably want to employ an attorney to process it, since this procedure can get to be quite complicated.

Here's the most important point to remember. There are time limitations on filing an appeal. For example, in New Jersey, traffic court appeals must generally be filed within ten days after the entry of judgment. In this case, you may have to make up your mind rather quickly if you want to proceed with an appeal. If you file too late, your appeal can be dismissed. In view of this, I suggest that you always make it a point to find out how much time you have as soon as you can. (Note: Probably the easiest way to do this is to simply ask the judge at the conclusion of your case.)

DEFINITIONS

Accused   (1) The person who has been charged with a traffic offense. (2) the defendant.

Admissible Evidence   Evidence that the judge allows to be considered in reaching the decision in the case.

Adversary   Anyone from the opposing side, such as the prosecutor.

Affidavit   A written statement made under oath.

Alibi   A defense that is based on the accused having been somewhere else at the time the offense was committed.

Annotations   Notes or comments intended to illustrate the meaning of something. These often follow the text of statutes or codes.

Appeal   The process whereby an appellate court reviews the decision of the lower court.

Appellate Court   A court to which cases are appealed.

Argument   This refers to the statements made in an effort to establish a defense.

BAC   Blood alcohol content.

Burden Of Proof   The necessity of establishing guilt by the requisite degree of proof.

Case Law   The aggregate of reported legal cases.

Charge   This term refers to any traffic offense that one is accused of.

Citation   See *Traffic Ticket.*

Complain   This refers to the act of accusing someone else of having committed a traffic offense.

Contempt   (1) An intentional disregard of a court order. (2) A showing of disrespect for the court.

Continuance   A postponement of a hearing to a future date.

Court   A term that is used to refer not only to the court-house but also the judge or other officers of the court.

Court Clerk   The individual who generally performs functions such as the scheduling of cases, as well as administering the payment of fines, etc.

Conviction   The result of a trial or hearing that ends in a finding of guilt.

Credibility   Believability.

Cross-Examination   The part of the trial where witnesses are questioned by the opposing side.

Defendant   See *Accused*.

Defense   That which is offered by the defendant in order to win his case.

Demonstrative Evidence   Evidence other than the testimony of witnesses, such as photographs or drawings.

Direct Examination   The part of the trial where witnesses are questioned by the side that calls them.

Discovery   The process of obtaining information from the state that relates to the case.

Discretion   The authority to exercise one's own decisions to a certain extent.

Dismissal   An order by the judge that terminates the case in favor of the defendant.

DMV   Department of Motor Vehicles.

DUI   Driving uner the influence.

DWS   Driving while suspended.

Element A term used to designate one of the parts that comprise a traffic offense.

Exhibit See *Demonstrative Evidence.*

Error This refers to any mistake a court makes during trial. If the error is prejudicial to the defendant's rights, it can constitute grounds for an appellate court to grant relief by upsetting the judgment.

Evidence Information that demonstrates the truth or falsehood of the point in issue.

Foundation The basis that is sometimes necessary before certain types of evidence can be admitted.

Guilty A plea whereby the defendant admits that he is responsible for the offense he is accused of.

Harmless Error An error that was not prejudicial to the defendant's rights and which does not constitute grounds for the appellate court to upset the decision of the lower court.

Hearing See *Proceeding*

Hypothetical Situation This refers to a set of circumstances that are based on assumed facts.

Inadmissible Evidence Evidence that the judge does not allow to be considered in reaching the decision in the case.

Incident The event or occurrence that led to the issuance of a traffic ticket.

Intent A state of mind whereby a person desires a particular result.

Irrebuttable Presumption A presumption that may not be disproved by the evidence.

Judge The official who hears cases in court.

Judgment The final decision given by the court.

Jurisdiction (1) The authority by which a court can exercise power over a person or a particular case. (2) A term used to designate a certain geographical area, such as the state of California.

Law (1) The whole body of statutes, rules, ordinances, etc. that must be followed by the population. (2) Any individual statute, rule, or ordinance.

Layperson Someone who does not belong to the legal profession.

Legal Justification The existence of circumstances that make it excusable to violate the law.

Legal Presumption A rule of law that says that the judge must draw a particular conclusion from certain evidence.

License Suspension A temporary deprivation of the privilege to drive.

Mitigating Circumstances Circumstances that may be considered in reducing the penalty for a traffic offense.

Motion The name given to the act of submitting a request to the judge.

Merger The absorption of one offense into another whereby one of the offenses ceases to exist.

No Contest Essentially the same as a plea of guilty with the exception that this plea may not usually be used as an admission of guilt in a civil proceeding.

Not Guilty A plea whereby the defendant does not admit responsibility for the offense he is accused of.

Objection An argument presented in opposition to some improper statement or action by the state.

Occurrence See *Incident.*

Offense A violation or breach of the traffic law.

Ordinance A law established by a municipality that applies locally as opposed to throughout a state.

Plea The answer given by the defendant to the charge.

Plea Bargaining A procedure for settling cases before trial.

Proceeding A court case.

Proof The result or effect of evidence.

Pro Se A Latin term that means in one's own behalf.

Prosecution A proceeding instituted by the state against someone who has violated the traffic law.

Prosecutor The individual who conducts the prosecution on behalf of the state.

Quasi-Criminal Similar in character to that of a criminal act.

Rebut To contradict or disprove.

Rebuttable Presumption A presumption that may be disproved by the evidence.

Regulations Rules issued by the government that deal with procedure.

Reversal The voiding or setting aside of something, such as when an appellate court overturns the decision of a lower court.

Reversible Error An error that constitutes grounds for the appellate court to upset the decision of the lower court.

Rule An established standard or regulation.

Speed Measurements The results of radar or other devices designed to measure the speed of motor vehicles.

Standard Of Proof The measure of proof required for the state to obtain a conviction, such as "beyond a reasonable doubt."

State A term which represents the body of people of any individual state (such as New York), who are considered wronged by a violation of the traffic law.

Statute A law established and enacted by the legislature.

Stipulation   An agreement between the prosecutor and the defendant (or his attorney) regarding some matter pertaining to the trial.

Subpoena   A formal written document which commands a person to appear in court.

Subpoena Duces Tecum   A subpoena that commands a witness to produce any documents or papers in his possession that may be pertinent to issues in the case.

Testimony   Oral evidence given by a witness.

Traffic Ticket   A document that contains a statement of the charge and a notice to appear.

Transcript   A copy of the record made of the court proceedings.

Trial   The formal examination of the case in issue by the court.

Valid   Justifiable.

Verdict   The formal decision made by a jury.

Violation   See *Offense.*

Waive   To give up or relinquish.

Witness   Someone who testifies to what he has seen, heard or observed.

APPENDIX A

BOOKS THAT DEAL WITH LEGAL RESEARCH

Cohen, Morris L. *Legal Research in a Nutshell.* 4th ed. (St. Paul, MN: West Publishing Company) 1985.

Honigsberg, Peter Jan *Legal Research and Writing.* 4th ed. (Chicago, IL: Harcourt Brace Jovanovich Legal and Professional Publications, Inc.) 1987.

Elias, Steven *Legal Research, How to Find and Understand the Law.* 2nd ed. (Berkeley, CA.: Nolo Press) 1986.

Wren, Christopher G., and Wren, Jill Robinson *The Legal Research Manual, A Game Plan for Legal Research and Analysis.* 2nd ed. (Madison, WI.: A-R Editions, Inc.) 1986.

APPENDIX B

SYMPTOMS PRODUCED BY ALCOHOL AND/OR OTHER PATHOLOGICAL CONDITIONS

National Safety Council
Committee on Tests for Intoxication

FLUSHED FACE
A Emotion
L Shyness
C Chlorosis
O Indigestion
H Feeble Circulation
O General Disability
L Epilepsy

DILATED PUPILS
A Tabes Dorsalis
L Aneurysm
C Atropine
O Catalepsy
H Fright
O Emotion
L Glaucoma
   Toxic Goiter
   Acute Mania

ATAXY
A Diptheria
L Disease of Spinal Cord
      Tabes Dorsalis
      Friederich's Ataxy
      Disseminated Sclerosis
      Syringomyelia
      New Growths or Tumors
C Lesions in Brain Stem
      Ocular Paralysis
O Lesion of Cerebrum
H Lesions of Cerebellum
      Tumors
      Thrombosis Cerb. art.
      Encephalitis
O Hysterical Ataxy
L Chorea

INCOORDINATION
A Tabes Dorsalis
L Ataxic Paraplegia
C Disseminated Sclerosis
O Hereditary Ataxy
H Cerebellar Disease
O Paralysis of Eye Muscles
L

CONTRACTED PUPILS
A Cerebral Tumor
L Cervical Symlesion
C Spinal Cord Lesion
O Encephalitis
H Hypermetropia
O Inter-Cranial Abscess
L Iritis
   Tabes Dorsalis
   Uremia
   Thyroid Gland Enlargement

SPEECH
A Slurred
      Disseminated Sclerosis
      Friederich's Disease
L Scanning
      Cerebellar Abscess
      Cerebellar Tumor
      Disseminated Sclerosis
C Defective
      Cerebral Embolism
      Diplegia
      Disseminated Sclerosis
      Chorea
      Delayed Development
O Loss of
      Pneumonia
H Typhoid Fever
O Migraine
      Hemiplegia
L Cerebral Syphilis

LOCAL LOSS OF POWER
A Pseudo Paralysis
L Congenital Dislocation of Hips
C Infantile Paralysis
O Old Nemi or Mono or
H Para-plegias
O
L

COMA COMES EARLY
A Results of Head Injury
      Concussion
      Concussion Meningeal Hemorrhage
      Depressed Fracture
      Fracture Base of Skull
L Vascular Lesion of Brain
      Embolism
      Hemorrhage
C Thrombosis, Arterial or Venous
      Acute Effect of Drugs:
      Opium   Veronal
O Morphine   Sulphonal
      Carbolic Acid   Trional
      Oxalic Acid   Barbital Group
H Carbon Monoxide   Bromides
      Absinthe   Anesthetics
      Chronic
      Lead Poisoning
O Heat Stroke
      Excessive Hemorrhage
      Ruptured Tubal Gestation
      Post-Partum Hemorrhage
L Haematemsis
      Intestinal Hemorrhage
      Stokes-Adams Disease
      Sudden Nervous Shock
      Hysterical Trance

137

SYMPTOMS PRODUCED BY ALCOHOL AND/OR OTHER PATHOLOGICAL CONDITIONS (continued)

COMA COMES LATE

A   Lesions of Brain or Meningitis
Suppurative Meningitis
T. B. C.
Posterior Basal Meningitis
L   Epidemic Cerebrospinal Meningitis
Acute Encephalitis
Lesions of Central Nervous System
C   Cerebral Tumor
Cerebral Abscess
Post-Epileptic State
O   General Paralysis of Insane
Disseminated Sclerosis
Syphilis of the Brain
H   Diseases of Metabolism
Uremia
O   Diabetes
Cholaemia
Addison's Disease
L   Raynaud's Disease
Myxoedema

APPENDIX C

SELECTED SECTIONS FROM THE NEW JERSEY ADMINISTRATIVE CODE

13:51-1.1 Purpose of subchapter

This subchapter prescribes the requirements for certification of a person to conduct chemical analysis of the breath of a person arrested pursuant to N.J.S.A. 39:4-50 et seq., N.J.S.A. 12:7-34.19, N.J.S.A. 12:7-46, N.J.S.A. 2A:4A-23, or N.J.S.A. 12:7-54 et seq., the conditions under which certification can occur and the general rules for holders of certificates, pursuant to the statutory requirements of L.1966, c.142, Sec. 3, as amended by L. 1971, c.273, Sec. 1 (C. 39:4-50.3); hereinafter denoted as N.J.S.A. 39:4-50.3 or L.1986, c.39, Sec. 8 (C. 12:7-56); hereinafter denoted as N.J.S.A. 12:7-56.

13:51-1.2 Definitions

For the purpose of this chapter, and subchapters 1, 2, and 3 thereof, the terms set forth herein are defined as follows:

"Approved instrument" shall mean a device or instrument approved by the Attorney General at N.J.A.C. 13:51-3.5 for use in the chemical analysis of the breath of a person arrested pursuant to the provisions of N.J.S.A. 39:4-50 et seq., N.J.S.A. 12:7-34.19, N.J.S.A. 12:7-6 or N.J.S.A. 2A:4A-23.

"Approved methods" shall mean those steps or operations approved by the Attorney General at N.J.A.C. 13:51-3.6 for use in the chemical analysis of the breath of a person arrested pursuant to the provisions of N.J.S.A. 39:4-50 et seq., N.J.S.A. 12:7-34.19, N.J.S.A. 12:7-46 or N.J.S.A. 2A:4A-23 on an approved instrument.

"Approved school" shall mean police training academies and schools as approved by the Police Training Commission pursuant to N.J.S.A. 52:17B-67, et seq. It shall also include the Training Academy of the Division of State Police and any similar such academy, training center or school operated by or for the Department of Defense of the United States of America.

"Breath Test Coordinator/Instructor" is a person who meets the eligibility requirements as set forth at N.J.A.C. 13:51-2 and is duly appointed thereunder.

"Calendar year" shall mean all days of a year commencing with and including January 1 of a specific year and continuing through to and including December 31 of the same year.

"Certification" shall mean the approval by the Attorney General of a person as an operator, as herein defined, and shall mean said person is qualified and competent to perform chemical breath test analysis utilizing an approved method and an approved instrument as defined in this subchapter and as set forth at N.J.A.C. 13:51-3 as authorized by N.J.S.A. 39:4-50.3 or N.J.S.A. 12:7-56.

"Operation of an approved instrument" shall mean operation of an approved instrument (as defined herein) by approved methods (as defined herein) for the operation of that approved instrument.

"Operator" shall mean a person who is certified as a Chemical Breath Test Operator to perform analysis of an arrested person's breath utilizing an approved method and an approved instrument, as defined in this subchapter and as set forth at N.J.A.C. 13:51-3 and pursuant to the provisions of N.J.S.A. 39:4-50.3 or N.J.S.A. 12:7-56.

"Operator's certificate" shall mean a certificate issued under the authority of the Attorney General which bears the signatures or facsimile signatures of the Attorney General and the Superintendent of State Police.

"Organized police department" shall include all police and law enforcement agencies of the State of New Jersey; and all municipal and county police agencies of the various municipalities and counties of the State of New Jersey as established by law; and police agencies established by the laws of the United States of America within the Department of Defense.

"Recertification" shall mean the extension of the certification of an operator upon compliance with the training as required by this subchapter.

"Replica" shall mean a document which is an operator's certificate as defined in this section and which shall bear the signatures or facsimile signatures of the Attorney General and the Superintendent of State Police and which is of a size that permits it to be carried in the pocket, purse, wallet, etc., and includes replacements thereof as set forth at N.J.A.C. 13:51-1.12(c).

"Satisfactory completion of training" shall mean demonstrated competence of operation of chemical breath test analysis methods and devices or instruments approved by the Attorney General as set forth at N.J.A.C. 13:51-3, maintenance of a passing course average and passing a written examination.

13:51-1.3   Certification

(a) For the purpose of prosecution, no operator may conduct a valid analysis of an arrested person's breath under the provisions of N.J.S.A. 39:4-50.3 or N.J.S.A. 12:7-56, unless such operator has been issued a valid operator's certificate which is current at the time of the analysis of an arrested person's breath and which attests that such operator is then qualified and competent to conduct such analysis utilizing an approved method and an approved instrument as set forth at N.J.A.C. 13:51-3.

(b) Certification of a person as an operator shall be by recommendation of the Superintendent of the State Police to the Attorney General upon the satisfactory completion of training as more fully set forth at N.J.A.C. 13:51-1.6.

13:51-1.4   Prerequisite for application for certification

An applicant for certification as an operator must be a sworn, full-time member of an organized police department for a minimum of one year after graduation from an approved school; except that members of a police or law enforcement agency of the Department of Defense of the United States of America may apply at any time after graduation from an approved school.

13:51-1.5   Application for operator's certification

Application shall be made in writing to the Division of State Police by the Chief of Police or other executive head of the organized police department of which the applicant is a sworn full-time member.

13:51-1.6   Requirements for certification

(a) Initial certification requires satisfactory completion of training consisting of a minimum of five days of training prescribed and conducted by the Division of State Police. Such training shall include:

1. Instruction in the metric system;
2. Instruction in mathematical calculations as required;
3. Statutory and case law;
4. Instruction and training in the operation of the approved instrument;
5. Laboratory practice with air samples passed through test solutions of alcohol and air samples taken from human subjects;
6. A written examination and a test for competency.

(b) Certification of an applicant upon an approved instrument other than that which the applicant was previously trained and certified, requires that the applicant be a certified breath test operator and whose certification is both current and valid and requires satisfactory completion of training consisting of a minimum of two days of training prescribed and conducted by the Division of State Police. Such training shall include:

1. Statutory and case law, instruction and training in the operation of the approved instrument;
2. Instruction and training in the operation of the approved instrument;
3. Laboratory practice with air samples passed through test solutions of alcohol;
4. A written test and a test for competency.

(c) A person who has received a post graduate degree from an institution of higher education in the field of chemistry or biochemistry or a person licensed as a doctor of medicine shall be deemed to have met the requirements of satisfactory completion of training and may be recommended for certification,

provided said person also passes a test for competency in the operation of the approved instrument as administered by a Breath Test Coordinator/Instructor of the Division of State Police.

(d) Recertification of an operator, whose certification is not subject to suspension for any reason or revoked, requires satisfactory completion of training consisting of a minimum one day of training as prescribed and conducted by the Division of State Police. Such training shall include:

1. Statutory and case law;
2. Instruction and training in the operation of the approved instrument;
3. Laboratory practice with air samples passed through test solutions of alcohol;
4. A written examination and a test for competency.

(e) Reinstatement and recertification of an operator whose certification is suspended pursuant to N.J.A.C. 13:51-1.8(a) and to whom the requirements as set forth at N.J.A.C. 13:51-1.8(b) apply requires satisfactory completion of training as set forth at N.J.A.C. 13:51-1.6(d).

(f) Reinstatement and special recertification of an operator whose certification is suspended pursuant to N.J.A.C. 13:51-1.8(a) and to whom the requirements as set forth at N.J.A.C. 13:51-1.8(c) apply requires satisfactory completion of training consisting of a minimum of three days of training prescribed and conducted by the Division of State Police. Such training shall include:

1. Statutory and case law;
2. Instruction and training in the operation of the approved instrument;
3. Laboratory practice with air samples passed through test solutions of alcohol;
4. A written examination and a test for competency.

13:51-1.7   Duration of certification

(a) An operator's certification will be documented by the issuance of a certificate and replica which shows that said operator has completed the required course of training, including the date of the course completion and type of approved instrument upon which the operator has been certified. Said certification as evidenced by the certificate and replica shall be valid throughout the remainder of the calendar year corresponding to the date of course completion and shall remain valid throughout the next two calendar years.

(b) An operator's certification will be deemed continued as valid upon the satisfactory completion of training for recertification as described at N.J.A.C. 13:51- 1.6(d). Recertification shall be valid throughout the remainder of the calendar year corresponding to the completion date of the recertification course and shall remain valid throughout the next two calendar years.

(c) The certification of an operator which has been suspended pursuant to N.J.A.C. 13:51-1.8(a) and who has been reinstated and recertified pursuant to N.J.A.C. 13:51-1.8(b) or N.J.A.C. 13:51-1.8(c) will be deemed to be valid for all purposes as of and from the date of reinstatement and recertification. This reinstatement and recertification shall thereafter be valid throughout the remainder of the calendar year corresponding to the date of reinstatement and recertification and shall remain valid throughout the next two calendar years.

(d) The recertification and/or reinstatement and recertification of an operator pursuant to N.J.A.C. 13:51-1.6(d), N.J.A.C. 13:51-1.6(e) or N.J.A.C. 13:51-1.6(f), whichever applies, is considered validated when the replica is signed and dated by a Breath Test Coordinator/Instructor.

13:51-1.8   Suspension and reinstatement of operator's certification

(a) The certification of an operator will be automatically suspended on the date set for expiration of the operator's present valid certification as set forth at N.J.A.C. 13:51-1.7 if said operator has not satisfied the requirement for recertification as set forth at N.J.A.C. 13:51-1.6(d) before the expiration of said valid certification.

(b) An operator whose certification is suspended for failing to be recertified as set forth at N.J.A.C. 13:51-1.6(d) and who has been automatically suspended for less than one year from the date of the automatic suspension must attend and satisfy the requirements of the reinstatement and recertification course as set forth at N.J.A.C. 13:51-1.6(e) conducted by the Division of State Police. Reinstatement and recertification under this subsection must be completed before one year from the date of automatic suspension otherwise the operator must satisfy the requirements as set forth at N.J.A.C. 13:51-1.8(c).

(c) An operator whose certification is suspended for failing to be recertified as set forth at N.J.A.C. 13:51-1.6(d) or N.J.A.C. 13:51-1.6(e) and who has been automatically suspended for one year or more from the date of the automatic suspension must attend and satisfy the requirements of a reinstatement and special recertification course as set forth at N.J.A.C. 13:51-1.6(f) conducted by the Division of State Police.

(d) Any test conducted to anaylze a person's breath pursuant to procedures and methods contained in this chapter by an operator whose certification is suspended or automatically suspended, at the time such test is conducted, shall be considered invalid for presentation in evidence or testimony in a court of law or administrative hearing.

13:51-1.9   Revocation of certificate

(a) The Attorney General may revoke an operator's certification after consideration of a request or recommendation for revocation by the Superintendent of State Police.

(b) A request or recommendation for revocation will be made to the Attorney General when an operator is determined to be ineffective or incompetent by the Superintendent of State Police.

(c) A request or recommendation that an operator's certification be revoked must be in writing and addressed to the Superintendent of State Police and must state the reason(s) for the request or recommendation for revocation. The replica certificate of the operator who is the subject of the request or recommendation must accompany the request or recommendation for revocation unless it is otherwise unobtainable.

(d) The following persons are authorized to initiate a request or recommendation for revocation:

1. A Breath Test Coordinator/Instructor; or

2. Chief of Police of the organized police department of which the operator is a sworn member; or

3. Executive head of the organized police department of which the operator is a sworn member.

(e) Upon receipt of a request or recommendation for revocation, the Superintendent of State Police shall cause a written Notice of Suspension to be delivered to the operator who is the subject of the request or recommendation. A copy of the Notice of Suspension shall also be delivered to the Chief of Police or executive head of the organized police department of which the operator is a sworn member. The Notice of Suspension shall state:

1. The effective date of suspension;

2. The reason(s) revocation has been requested or recommended;

3. The name and title of the person originating the request or recommendation for revocation; and

4. Information that the operator may request a hearing on the request or recommendation for revocation by serving the Superintendent of State Police with written notice of such request within 30 days of the date the notice of suspension was signed and dated by the Superintendent of State Police.

(f) Failure to request a hearing as set forth at N.J.A.C. 13:51-1.9(e) within the time allotted shall be considered an absolute waiver of any right to a hearing.

13:51-1.10   Hearing and determination on a request or recommendation for revocation

(a) The purpose of a hearing is to assist the Superintendent of State Police in arriving at a determination on the request or recommendation for revocation as set forth at N.J.A.C. 13:51-1.9(b). Where no hearing is conducted the Superintendent of State Police may make his determination based on the written documentation supplied in the request or recommendation to revoke or other materials supplied in support or opposition thereto.

(b) The hearing will be conducted by the Superintendent of State Police or by an officer designated by him. The hearing officer may, at his discretion, cause the operator to be given a written or oral examination or a competency test or any combination of such tests to arrive at a determination. Such tests may be given by a Breath Test Coordinator/Instructor or other person so designated by the Superintendent or the hearing officer.

(c) Upon conclusion of the hearing or review when no hearing is requested, the Superintendent of State Police will recommend, in writing, to the Attorney General whether the operator's certification should be revoked, including the reasons to support such recommendation; or if the operator's certification should be reinstated and the reasons in support thereof. Reinstatement may be conditioned upon the suspended operator satisfying certain training or other requirements. The Attorney General shall determine, in his sole discretion, what conditions or other requirements must be met before reinstatement can become effective.

(d) An operator recommended for reinstatement with conditions or other requirements as set forth at N.J.A.C. 13:51-1.10(c), who fails to satisfy and successfully complete said conditions or other requirements within a reasonable period of time, may be recommended by the Superintendent of State Police to the Attorney General for revocation of the operator's certification.

3:51-1.11   Restoration of revoked certifications

The Attorney General may restore a revoked certification when he is satisfied that the cause for revocation has been removed. An operator whose certification is revoked may apply for a new operator's certification after the expiration of 12 months from the date of revocation, or final judgment thereon, whichever is later. Application shall be pursuant to the provisions of N.J.A.C. 13:51-1.4 and N.J.A.C. 13:51-1.5, but shall be subject to review by the Superintendent of State Police. The applicant must complete the training as set forth at N.J.A.C. 13:51-1.6(a); but may not commence such training until any other requirements imposed by the Superintendent of State Police are satisfied. Upon satisfactory completion of training and any other prerequisites, the Superintendent of State Police may recommend certification of the applicant to the Attorney General.

3:51-1.12 Return, loss and/or replacement of replica

(a) If an operator's certification is suspended or revoked pursuant to N.J.A.C. 13:51-1.9 and/or N.J.A.C. 13:51-1.10, or if the operator resigns, retires or leaves the police department for any reason, it shall be the responsibility of the Chief of Police or other executive head of the organized police department or law enforcement agency where the operator serves or served to retrieve the replica certificate from the operator and return the same to the Division of State Police with a notation of the reason for the return.

(b) If a replica has been lost or is otherwise in need of replacement, the operator or Chief of Police or other executive head of the organized police department of which the operator is a member shall notify the Breath Test Unit of the Division of State Police in writing of such loss or need of replacement. Lost replicas must be reported immediately.

(c) A replica will be replace for an operator when the operator's replica has been lost and duly reported as lost, pursuant to N.J.A.C. 13:51-1.12(b) or is otherwise in need of replacement. The replacement replica will bear the date of issuance of the replacement and bear the signatures or facsimile signatures of the Attorney General and the Superintendent of State Police. The reverse side of the replacement replica will show the date of the operator's original certification and the date of the operator's most recent recertification.

13:51-1.13 Administration

Administrative files will be maintained by the Division of State Police and will include the present and past status of all persons certified as operators.

13:51-2.1 Eligibility requirements

(a) To be eligible as a Breath Test Coordinator/Instructor a person must be a sworn member of the New Jersey State Police, hold a current and valid Breath Test Certificate and be a holder of:

1. A certificate in police training issued by the New Jersey Police Training Commission; or

2. An instructor certificate issued by the United States Armed Forces; or

3. Certification from a duly accredited school of education; or

4. Instructor certificate issued by the Division of State Police, Training Bureau.

(b) The Attorney General may waive the instructor certification requirement, if he is satisfied such person has equivalent background and experience to instruct breath test applicants and operators.

(c) The Attorney General's approval will be in the form of a letter to the person approved as a Breath Test Coordinator/Instructor and will be reflected on the operator's replica certificate by the words Breath Test Coordinator/Instructor.

13:51-2.2 Training and functional qualifications

(a) A Breath Test Coordinator/Instructor will have specialized training as prescribed by the Division of State Police and have the knowledge to properly perform the following functions:

1. Preparation and checking of chemicals used for testing;

2. Presentation of the scientific theory of approved instruments and approved methods;

3. Inspection and maintenance of approved instruments;

4. Instruction in courses for operators and applicants;

5. Make a request or recommendation for revocation of an operators certification;

6. Validate replica certificates held by certified breath test operators as provided at N.J.A.C. 13:51-1.7 (Duration of certification).

13:51-3.1 Purpose of subchapter

Pursuant to the provisions of L.1966, c.142, Sec. 3, as amended by L.1971 c.273, Sec. 1 (C. 39:4-50.3), and L.1986, c.39, Sec. 8 (C. 12:7-56); hereinafter denoted N.J.S.A. 39:4-50.3 or N.J.S.A. 12:7-56, respectively, the provisions of this subchapter set forth the instruments and methods approved by the Attorney General for the chemical analysis of the breath of a person arrested pursuant to the provisions of N.J.S.A. 39:4-50, et seq., N.J.S.A. 12:7-34.19, N.J.S.A. 12:7-46 or N.J.S.A. 2A:4A-23.

13:51-3.2 Application for approval

(a) The Superintendent of State Police is designated by the Attorney General as the official to whom all applications for approval of instruments, methods and operational functions shall be made.

(b) Primarily, evaluation will be dependent upon test results reflecting reliability for satisfactory specificity, precision and accuracy. The instrument and component parts necessary for operation shall be supplied at the expense of the applicant.

(c) Any evaluating reports by the applicant or independent investigating groups shall be forwarded with the instrument along with operating servicing and maintenance manuals, schematic drawings and other detailed information.

(d) Upon completion of evaluation of an instrument, method and/or operational function, the Superintendent shall recommend approval or rejection of the same to the Attorney General. The Attorney General, upon review of the recommendations, shall approve or reject the instrument, method and/or operational function pursuant to law (N.J.S.A. 39:4-50.3 or N.J.S.A. 12:7-56).

13:51-3.3 Training Breath Test Coordinator/Instructors

(a) Upon approval of an instrument, method and/or operational function as described in N.J.A.C. 13:51-3.2, factory personnel shall train an initial class consisting of Breath Test Coordinator/Instructors (see N.J.A.C. 13:51-2) at the expense of the applicant.

(b) The initial training course shall include the history of the instrument, nomenclature of the operational controls, detailed operating instructions, nomenclature of all parts and their functions, maintenance and repair of the instrument and class participation in the operation of the device including laboratory practice with air passed through test solutions of alcohol of strengths known and unknown to the class participants.

13:51-3.4 Periodic inspection of approved instruments

Periodic inspection of all approved instruments used in this State in connection with the prosecution of a person pursuant to the provisions of N.J.S.A. 39:4-50 et seq., N.J.S.A. 12:7-34.19, N.J.S.A. 12:7-46 or N.J.S.A. 2A:4A-23 shall be made by a Breath Test Coordinator/Instructor. The results of such periodic inspections shall be recorded on forms provided by the Superintendent of State Police and the originals thereof shall be maintained by the Division of State Police.

13:51-3.5 Approved instruments for performing chemical analysis of a person's breath

(a) The Breathalyzer, Model 900, is an instrument approved by the Attorney General pursuant to L. 1966 c.142, Sec. 3, as amended by L. 1971 c.273, Sec. 1 (C. 39:4-50.3) and L. 1986 c.39, Sec. 8 (C. 12:7-56) and this subchapter, for the testing of a person's breath by chemical analysis.

(b) The Breathalyzer, Model 900A, is an instrument approved by the Attorney General pursuant to L. 1966 c.142, Sec. 3, as amended by L. 1971 c.273, Sec. 1 (C. 39:4-50.3) and L. 1986 c.39, Sec. 8 (C. 12:7-56) and this subchapter, for the testing of a person's breath by chemical analysis.

(c) The Dominator Albreath is an instrument approved by the Attorney General pursuant to L. 1966 c.142, Sec. 3, as amended by L. 1971 c.273, Sec. 1 (C. 39:4-50.3) and L. 1986 c.39, Sec. 8 (C. 12:7-56) and this subchapter, for the testing of a person's breath by chemical analysis.

(d) The Alco-Tector is an instrument approved by the Attorney General pursuant to L. 1966 c.142, Sec. 3, as amended by L. 1971 c.273, Sec. 1 (C. 39:4-50.3) and L. 1986 c.39 Sec. 8 (C. 12:7-56) and this subchapter, for the testing of a person's breath by chemical analysis.

Amended by R.1985 d.441, effective September 3, 1985.
See: 17 N.J.R. 1531(a), 17 N.J.R. 2141(b).
    Deleted (e).
Amended by R.1987 d.229, effective May 18, 1987.
See: 19 N.J.R. 444(b), 19 N.J.R. 882(b).
    Added N.J.S.A. cites.

13:51-3.6 Approved methods for performing chemical analysis of a person's breath utilizing an approved instrument

(a) Breathalyzer, Model 900 and Model 900A:

1. The Breathalyzer, Model 900 and 900A, both being approved instruments, have been demonstrated to contain functional and operational components that are the same or perform the same or similar operations or functions and operate utilizing the same principal or theory of chemical

breath analysis and utilize the same chemical compounds interchangeably in the analysis process. The term "Breathalyzer" as utilized in this chapter shall mean both the Breathalyzer, Model 900 and Model 900A.

i. Any operator or Breath Test Coordinator/Instructor whose certificate specifies Breathalyzer is deemed trained and certified on the Breathalyzer Model 900 and Breathalyzer, Model 900A.

2. A Breathalyzer check off list may be used with this device and may be prepared by either the manufacturer of the Breathalyzer or the organization using the Breathalyzer. The check off list, if used, shall contain at least the following items:

i. **Preparation:**

(1) Turn Switch to "on"; wait until thermometer shows 50 degrees Centigrade plus or minus three degrees;

(2) Gauge reference ampoule and place in left hand holder;

(3) Gauge test ampoule; open; insert bubbler and connect to outlet.

ii. **Purge:**

(1) Turn to "take"; flush; turn to "analyze";

(2) When red empty signal appears, wait 90 seconds, turn on light, balance.

iii. **Analysis:**

(1) Set scale Pointer on start line;

(2) Turn to "take"; take breath sample; turn to "analyze";

(3) When red empty signal appears, wait 90 seconds, turn on light; balance;

(4) Record answer; dispose of test ampoule; turn to "off".

(b) Dominator Albreath:

1. The Dominator Albreath, being an approved instrument, has been determined to contain operational and functional components that are the same or perform the same or similar operations or functions as the Breathalyzer as described at N.J.A.C. 13:51-3.6(a)1. It is further determined that this instrument operates upon the same principal or theory as the Breathalyzer and utilize the same chemical compounds in the analysis process as the Breathalyzer.

2. The steps of operation in the check off list applicable to the Breathalyzer as found at N.J.A.C. 13:51-3.6(a)2 shall also apply to the operation of the Dominator Albreath when a check off list is employed.

(c) Alco-Tector:

1. The Alco-Tector, being an approved instrument, has been determined to operate on the same basic principle or theory and utilizes the same chemical compounds in the analysis process as the Breathalyzer as described at N.J.A.C. 13:51-3.6(a)1.

2. An operational check off list may be used with this device and may be prepared by either the manufacturer of the Alco-Tector or the organization using the Alco-Tector. The check off list, if used and prepared by an organization other than the manufacturer herein, shall contain, at least, the following information:

i. **Preparation:**

(1) Turn switch to "on", depress standby button, wait for thermometer to reach operating temperature of 120 to 130 degrees Fahrenheit;

(2) Gauge reference ampoule and place in left holder;

(3) Gauge test ampoule, open, insert bubbler, connect to outlet.

ii. Purge:

(1) Depress purge button number 1 for flush, wait 30 or 45 seconds, depress bubbler button number 2;

(2) When red empty signal appears, wait 90 seconds, depress balance button number 3 and balance.

iii. Analysis:

(1) Set blood alcohol pointer on start line;

(2) Depress sample button number 4, take breath sample, depress bubbler button number 5, record time;

(3) When red empty signal appears, wait 90 seconds, depress read button number 6 and balance;

(4) Record answer; dispose of test ampoule, depress number 1 button for 30 to 45 seconds, depress number 2 button until red light appears, depress standby button.

INDEX

NOTES